Execution by Firing Squad:

Effective Leadership When You're the Target

Dr. Philip Hickman

Dedication

I would like to thank God for the strength to stand in the fiery furnace and the lion's den to walk out unscathed. I dedicate this book to my family; especially my children Jaylen, Josiah, and Daniel for your patience and belief in me through it all.

A special thanks to my son, Jaylen, for being strong even though you had to change schools and states during your senior year of high school. You are amazing and an inspiration to me of ever enduring love and dedication.

Acknowledgment

I would like to acknowledge the teachings of Dr. Bob Thompson for impacting my leadership and this book.

About the Author

Dr. Philip Hickman is a true transformational leader in K-12 education and technology. Dr. Hickman is the Founder / CEO of MindAble Solutions, LLC and PlaBook. He has successfully developed two nonprofits that significantly impact education. He co-founded Mississippi Coding Academies and Learn Techquity in Kansas City, Missouri. Dr. Hickman is a prominent real estate developer and co-founder of Kell[ ]Man Development Corp. Dr. Hickman was a Superintendent and has received national recognition for his visionary integration of technology, personalization, and instructional transformation. He is only one of six U.S. Department of Education National Ambassadors. He is an author of the book "Stop Dribbling Footballs".

Dr. Hickman invented a new education instructional model called K-16 Instructional and Technology Integration Model (K-16 ITI Model) that is transforming teaching and personalizing learning within the classroom. Dr. Hickman's obsession with personalized learning fuels his partnership with the United States Department of Education on the #GoOpen movement or Openly License Educational Recourses (OER). Philip is an AASA Nationally Certified Superintendent.

Dr. Hickman has served diverse student populations and has led key reform initiatives across the nation in key leadership positions. Dr. Philip Hickman has previously served as the Assistant Superintendent as well as Area Superintendent for Houston Independent School District. Which is the seventh largest school district in the nation with about 289 schools and serving around 210,000 students. He has served as an adjunct professor at several universities. Philip was Director of Education in Kansas

City, Missouri and an educational advisor for a Missouri Senator. He has been a principal Illinois. He also worked as the assistant principal, dean of students, counselor, and school psychologist. Philip was a school psychologist for the Saint Louis County Special School District, also a special educator and student advocate in Columbia, Missouri.

Dr. Philip Hickman received his Bachelor of Arts (BA) in Psychology with a minor in Speech Pathology from the University of Missouri-Columbia. Philip has a Master of Arts in Education (M.Ed.) and an Educational Specialist (Ed.S.) in School Psychology from the University of Missouri- Columbia. He also studied at Southern Illinois University-Edwardsville receiving a Masters (M.Ed.) in Educational Administration. Philip continued his education at Saint Louis University receiving an Educational Specialist Degree (Ed.S) and a Doctor of Education (Ed.D.) with emphasis in Educational Leadership.

 @DrPWVHickman   Drphilip_hickman

 Philip Hickman   Dr. Philip Hickman

Preface

Dr. Philip Hickman commands respect in America's educational circles, thanks in no part to his formal training, steep accolades, and vast experience. For years, he has been at the front of fighting for children's education, believing that our students need to be the focus of our school system.

After going through a particularly horrible experience as a superintendent for a Mississippi school district, a tale which he recounts in the first section of this book, he became more determined to pursue this mission to bring innovation and leadership to American schools. On this quest, Dr. Hickman has gathered vital tips and advice for educators, parents, officials, academia, professors and leaders in any industry .

You will find all of this information packed into this one convenient book.

This work is divided into three distinct sections. Section I is an in-depth account of Dr. Hickman's journey and his personal experience. Section II encapsulates pragmatic leadership advice that includes a plethora of quotations that can be readily implemented in any setting.

Section III is a research-based exploration of leadership principles and proven models.

Foreword

Eric Thomas and Stephen Edwards Covey have made more than a few valuable contributions to the worlds of education and business. Their words have inspired many; however, I think it is safe to say that some of the most famous words of wisdom were: *"The main thing is to keep the main thing the main thing."* In other words, do not lose sight of that which is the most important.

When it comes to education, both Dr. Thomas and Mr. Covey knows exactly what the most important thing is — the students. They also know that the best method to accomplish this is to make sure each student understands that they are valued individuals with the potential to reach their own personal greatness.

As an educator I whole-heartedly adopt this philosophy as I know how important it is for students to receive the absolute best instruction, training, and opportunities that are available irrespective of their color, t socio-economic status, attitudes of the community, or even the implicit biases of the people charged with educating them. For these reasons, I am impassioned with making sure that education happens...*correctly*. In other words, I am deeply passionate about keeping the main thing, the main thing. Still, despite my desire to ensure leadership priorities were aligned with my passions and principles, there was a time not too terribly long ago when my passion for equality in education led to battles in my private and professional life. I would have never imagined that I would have to fight for my life, my career and the students to whom I dedicated my life's mission to serve. Not only did these battles attack my professionalism and knowledge as a leader, but they also brought me in the direct crosshairs of racial hostility against both me and the impoverished and minority children in the system. I was confronted with death threats, complete falsehoods and personal character assassination as I led the way towards ending the cycle of corruption, bribery, and neglect that negatively impacted the District's children.

These attacks were meant to destroy my character, my reputation, my desire to work for children, my personal life, and my confidence as a leader. However, these attempts failed terribly: I was able to lead my team of teachers and principals to accomplish unprecedented victories for students and assist a failing district in becoming ranked and progressive in the utilization of technology.

While it would be a far-stretch to say my race had nothing to do with the events you are about to "witness" (we're talking about the deep south, after all), it would be dishonest to say that the color of my skin was the *only* reason I ended up in front of their professional firing squad. So, what put me in the throes of this unwarranted war between the organization I was hired to lead and me? Four things can best sum up the answer to that question: (1) laziness (on the part of executives), (2) complacency (with the system), (3) greed, and (4) deep-rooted racial and social prejudices. In the succeeding chapters, you will see all of the details from the viewpoint of these four factors. You will see that the events that took place were built upon a culture of impropriety fueled by hatred and complacency.

Nonetheless, I have a story that I feel compelled to tell because the school district I was hired to lead could not and would not accept the fact that: a) I was an "outsider", b) I was not a "yes" man, c) I was one who refused to allow the continuance of grossly sub-standard practices, and d) I was not going to continue a tradition of divestment against the district's 90% impoverished and minority population.

As you read my story and what follows that, I want you to take the following keys from it:

- Students should always be the top priority in every school district;

- It is unacceptable to settle for anything less than the best available when it comes to providing resources and opportunities for students to learn and develop academically, socially, and individually;

- Every student, *EVERY* student, deserves equal access and opportunities to *EVERY* resource available; and

- A failing system is designed to fail and without proper reconstruction of that system, it will continue to fail.

It is also my desire that you walk away from reading my personal story with a determination to not give up as a leader or as a community, to be laser-focused on the constituency you serve and to foster a passion for advocating for them. Society deserves it, but more importantly, they deserve it.

Contents

Section I
My Leadership Story

Chapter 1
Taking 'It' Out for a Spin

I still remember that all-important day when I received the call as I was sitting in my office (my office in one of the top ten largest school districts in the United States). We were a district with just under 300 schools and approximately 210,000 students. My position as assistant superintendent of the district was one in which I was very proud. At the "ripe old age" of 34, I was one of the younger persons in my profession to have already reached that level in my career; something I did not take for granted. But I also knew that I was not done yet.

I wanted to go farther—much farther—than this and achieve more in the field. In part, this was due to the excellent mentorship and support of my boss. He was never one to try to hold me back for selfish reasons; but rather he genuinely wanted me to excel and succeed, with *absolutely* no ulterior motives. So, when I went to him to tell him that I wanted to "take my career out for a spin" by applying to superintendent positions, he wished me all the best. But, as with any good mentor, he also warned me to be cautious and to be prepared for the possibility that *some* organizations might still have the mindset that a minority might not be capable of leading a diverse group of constituents that included teachers and students, no matter how many degrees he or she had obtained nor the institution from which he or she received those degrees. He further explained that, nationally, the average superintendent lasted for approximately two-and-a-half years in any one position.

After assuring him (and myself) that I was up to the task of holding such a position *and* was ready to excel in the interview process necessary to make promotion happen, I started putting myself and my resume out there. It did not take long before people started calling me to set up interviews. Out of all the calls, there was one in which I was most interested—a large and very prominent school district in the state of Arizona.

The district was highly conservative, affluent, and with a 90% Caucasian student population. In other words, inviting diversity into the district did not appear to be at the top of their to-do list. Still, they could not ignore the fact that I was coming from a highly respected district, that I had the endorsement of my superiors and co-workers, and that I had already garnered several awards for excellence and achievements in the field. That being said, I made it through the elimination rounds and was selected as one of the final *two* contenders for the position. After a final round of interviews and a vote by the school board, I was offered the position. I was excited! I had just landed a dream position in a very prominent and progressive district. However, just days after I accepted the offer, I was informed that one of the members of the school board had called a *special meeting*. I was informed that this person had decided to do a little more digging into my background which revealed a photo of me posing with Barack Obama on my Facebook page.

The photo had been taken at an event while I was working in Chicago; but instead of viewing it as demonstrative of my achievements, this particular board member chose to use it as "proof" of my political views and agenda. He used the photo to stir up emotions and incite a mob-like reaction amongst the other board members. In the end, he called for another vote — one could say a "re-vote" but that would be illegal, but instead they were very savvy about how they re-evaluated my application and resume. The board used the *special meeting* as an open discussion forum; inviting parents and everyone else in the community that was concerned about local students.

The *special meeting* was called to order and the agenda focused on me. Taking center-stage at the meeting, this particular board member's rhetoric got everyone riled up, convincing just about everyone that I was a liberal who would be focused on changing the family values they had instilled in their children if I were selected. He further postulated that if I became the superintendent of *their* district, my supposed "love for Obama" would be the beginning of the end for the values and morals upon which their community was built.

Ultimately, a motion was made to vote on the contract offer to me. The vote was taken…they withdrew their offer to me and hired the other finalist. I was understandably upset and disappointed about this rescission of the offer of employment because I knew, beyond a shadow of a doubt, that I was qualified for the position and that I had a lot to offer to that community and its students. I also knew their reasons for withdrawing the offer were completely unfounded and erroneous, if not in itself, racist. But, even with this knowledge, I could have sold ocean-front property

4

in Missouri before I would have been able to convince them of that reality. If it had been an option, they would have given the position to me before convening the *special meeting* and entertaining a new vote on the same issue. They would have given me a chance to defend myself against the accusations made against me and allowed me to prove my value to the school board and those with a vested interest in the students. However, that did not happen, so I had to move on. It was a heartbreaking decision but at the same time, this particular incident was also a blatant reminder of the warning issued to me by my mentor. Sure, theoretically, I knew it was possible, but I then had to face it head-on and I have to say, it was not a pretty reality. On a more positive note, I was empowered to know that not everyone in the community was happy about the decision that was made to rescind the offer of employment to me; the fact that the district was 90% white did NOT mean it was 90% against hiring a black superintendent. Indeed, the phone calls and messages I received from those who supported me in that community meant a lot to me. It was encouraging to know that not everyone was willing to be blindly led by those in positions of power.

Just as before the Arizona offer, offers started pouring in when word got around that I was not going to take the position in Arizona. It was a bit overwhelming (and quite flattering) because it was uncommon for a person whose job offer had just been rescinded to still be seen as valuable in the education job market. Still, I wanted to be careful to make the right choice for me and my family, as well as to set a proper course for my career (especially since this was my second at-bat). With all the offers, however, I knew it was possible to get distracted from being a focused leader, so I sat down and had a long conversation with my mentor.

I recall vividly his advice to me. He said,

You are a mission-driven leader. You are not meant to just sit in a big district chair and administer at the age that you are. You have the capability and desire to help children and lead communities; and now you also have the opportunity to give children something a lot of students will never have — a quality superintendent who will work in and out of the trenches to give them a higher quality of education than ever thought possible. You also have the ability and drive to lead teachers...not just oversee their job performance. You have the ability and drive to change the trajectory of the outcome of students' education wherever you go which will impact their future. All in all, you have the ability and drive.

Wow! Talk about feeling humble, proud, and full of purpose all at the same time. I was proud and thankful that he had seen these qualities in me because they are the very qualities I believe I personally bring to the table. To know I was actually demonstrating them in my day-to-day job by simply being myself was a huge "pat on the back". It was also the kind of affirmation I needed. I needed to know that someone who mattered (i.e. a more seasoned superior) recognized my abilities and my intentions. Yet, at the same time, his words humbled me and made me feel full of purpose. I was humbled by the fact that a man of his caliber had taken the time to pay that much attention to how I was doing my job and to understand me on a personal basis.

After this meeting, I fully intended to make sure that I did not drop the ball; that whomever I interviewed with would see these same qualities in me *and* that I would be able to live up to them as a superintendent.

After several interviews and considering all of my offers, I chose a district in the state of Mississippi. This district was amongst the poorest performing cities in the state and in fact, it was in the process of being taken over by the state because of its failing performance in special education, finance, and academic standing. In choosing to accept this position, I believed that I would have a greater impact in such a district because the changes would be noticeable and not par for the course. I also felt that it would impact the students in a more meaningful way. In fact, the following statistics were given to me in preparation of my arrival:

- The community population identified as 60% Caucasian, but the District's student population was 90% African-American;

- The economic status of the median household revealed that 98% of the entire student body qualified for free lunch (not free or reduced lunch... just free);

- Due to the federal poverty guidelines and severely sub-par academic achievement levels in the past 10 years, the bar was set at an LD level for the students;

- Desks and other furniture and fixtures had not been updated or replaced since the 1970s;

- The computer labs had consisted of three computers with CRT monitors (box monitors) that were at least 10 years old with only 2/3 in working condition. NOTE: By the time I was selected as superintendent, the manufacturer of these District computers had folded.

- Academic and athletic infrastructure of the student facilities were in disrepair (including classrooms, bathrooms, etc.);

- Electrical circuits that would allow for technological advancements were not in place; and

- Textbooks were outdated or did not meet the core requirements of the grade-level curriculum set by the State of Mississippi.

Based on the preceding information, even before I officially accepted the position, I knew there would be quite a few challenges; however, once I was stepped into the role of superintendent of the neglected and underperforming organization (which also happened to be in one of the lowest performing states in the United States), I found out I would not just be taking my professional abilities out for a spin, no, I immediately found out that I was going to be in the race of a lifetime that would dramatically challenge and change my ideas of leadership.

Chapter 2
First Things First

As an educational leader, I know that if you go into a district that is working well or even thriving, you leave it alone. Like the old adage goes, *"If it's not broken, do not try to fix it."* But if, on the other hand, the district you are assigned to is dysfunctional and underperforming, one needs to start repairing the most immediate issues before the damage gets any worse. I found myself in the latter situation.

I was not afforded the luxury of time. I did not have time for a 90-day plan that would typically consist of 60 days to observe and identify the source of the problem(s). The fact that the State of Mississippi was in the process of taking over this particular district was proof enough for me that the organization was in a dire state of emergency.

However, this damage had not happened overnight, so I knew there was quite a bit of work to be done to assess the source of the issue. The biggest problem I was facing right off the bat was time. I was onboarded literally days before the school year was supposed to start. Students are the central focus of any educational system, so they needed to become the main thing. As such, I decided the first order of business had to be the curriculum and textbooks. After all, that was the impetus for the existence and the purpose for which the students were attending.

Nonetheless, in order for the proper learning to take place, students had to have access to materials that would actually provide the information for which they would be held accountable. The Interim Superintendent had ordered textbooks, but they had not been delivered by the time I arrived. I was, however, able to get my hands-on copies of the books she had purchased (to the tune of several million dollars). Immediately, I began to review each of these textbooks; and to my surprise, I found that not one of them met the State curriculum guidelines and were not anywhere near the appropriate level for the students. I advised each school principals to leave the books sealed once they arrived — we were sending them back.

There was some confusion about my directives to send the books back, however, although this may come as a shock, I explained that it was not necessary that students have *physical* textbooks. I elaborated to my principals and teachers that in my research and experience, I found that a

11

growing number of educational systems (from elementary to post-secondary institutions) were exchanging textbooks for tablets. In fact, I was part of one of the first successful upgrades of this kind in my previous roles.

Here is why: using tablets was far more cost-effective for schools since only *one* tablet was needed for every subject and any peripheral lab or learning module needed, while on the other hand, having a physical textbook for every subject, was far more cost burdensome (as I stated previously, it is no secret how expensive that would have been). Some other benefits were that tablets were easier for the students to keep track, maintain, and was a piece of equipment in which they could take pride. Additionally, I felt that tablets were more than *just* academics. Tablets allowed students to gain technical skills, study skills, responsibility and accountability. Lastly (practically speaking), tablets were proven to be a health benefit to students by alleviating stress and strain on a student's posture and skeletal structure than were traditional textbooks. The icing on this cake was that by sending the textbooks back, I was able to repurpose the funds to purchase a tablet for every student in the district without adding a single penny to the budget. I was pumped! Here I was, the new kid on the block, and right out of the gate, I was going to be able to go to my school board and tell them how we were going to be able to take a HUGE *first* step in turning things around for students. In the process, the teachers would have a plethora of curriculum resources that were previously unavailable to them.

You can imagine how shocked I was when they responded to the announcement with anger and hostility. According to them, these kids did not need computers. They needed books, papers, and pencils. I explained to them that times were changing and that because of these shifts, it was getting harder to find textbooks that were able deliver the same quality of curriculum that we could get using tablets. I further explained that the tablets were essentially digital textbooks and online resources, all in one. I further elaborated that in order to remain relevant and up-to-date, upgrading to tablets was essential for bringing the students into the 21st century (of which we were already 10 years in). They were still extremely resistant. Somebody yelled at me during a board meeting, *"Dr. Hickman, you know what your problem is? You want to give these kids a Cadillac when they deserve a Chevy!"* I waited for a reaction because other members of the public were also in the room, but all I saw were people shaking their heads in agreement. I was absolutely shocked!

As a result of this fiasco at the board meeting, I decided to convene a public meeting. I thought that if I could get the parents on my side, the board would go with it. Surprisingly, the public meeting was as challenging as the board meeting, but for me personally, it was also heartbreaking. The parents just did not get it. They did not seem to understand the importance of bringing their students up to the same level as other students across the nation.

They did not understand that their children needed to be able to compete on a national level when it came to test scores, SAT/ACT scores, college entrance exams, and the like. They honestly believed that as long as their kids were doing better than the kids in the next *county* (which, by the way, was THE poorest county in the U.S.) things were "good" for them. They believed that outperforming a neighboring county with equal or worse performance was the best they could (or should) hope for. They even asked me to stop implying that their children had to compete globally against others for future jobs. Their attitude and outlook for their children and MY students shook me. It frustrated me, saddened me, and angered me.

Why and how had these parents come to believe that just because they were living at or below the federal poverty level, and just because their skin was black or brown, that their kids did not have a right to or were not expected to do their best? I knew that I had to turn the focus to the children. I knew that if I did not get this done, nothing else I did would really matter. It had also become blatantly apparent that no matter what I said or did, it would be in the face of intense opposition, even if it was in their best interest.

I was not deterred and eventually, we were able to purchase the tablets and put them into the hands of students. It should not have been such a feat. It should have been a simple yet important step forward — one that I believed the school board and parents should have embraced wholeheartedly. Unfortunately, it was not. Still, this was only the first of many battles and my first peek into what an organization full of nepotism and corruption looked like. This was my first look at an organization designed for the adult employees, and not its primary product or customers (i.e. the students). What I found was that this organization was designed to fail from the get-go.

Chapter 3
A Sad, Sad State of Affairs

Once the *Tablet vs. Textbook* issue settled, I continued assessing the overall health of the district to understand what would be necessary to start the process of moving forward and ultimately providing students with what they needed and deserved.

Next on the agenda: fact-gathering and data analysis of our District student performance against the State guidelines for performance.

Below were some key results from the analysis:

- The highest percentage of students in the District's highest performing school achieving the State minimum requirements was at 30%; and

- The lowest percentage of students in the District's lowest performing school who were achieving at the minimum state requirements was 10%.

What this information explained was that the District principals and teachers that were hired to lead and inspire students were failing (and miserably so). The very people who were supposed to be teaching students and equipping them to realize their full potential...*weren't*. Unfortunately, just like the students, their teaching GPAs were in the D and F range.

The next thing I found substantially related to underperformance was that tax revenue generated for the schools were being diverted to ***private schools*** which caused an unnecessary financial strain on the public educational systems. NOTE: I will talk more about this later, because this information was something I was not aware of until I was several months into year one of the four-year contract. I knew something had to be done to fix this and this would ultimately prove to be one of my biggest battles; but I just was not sure if or when I could tackle this issue.

Another alarming result of the investigatory analysis was that:

- When students entered kindergarten, 60% were at grade level;

- By the time those same students reached the 7th grade, only 20% were at described as being at grade level;

- By the time those same students reached high school, *less than 10%* were at grade level and were able to pass the 8th grade national math and reading assessments.

These statistics were included in my report to the board which also included the request to expend the textbook budget on tablets instead. As I said earlier, I was certain this report would be met with the same level of concern I had. Unfortunately, it was anything but that. One father even accused me of calling his daughter "stupid". I assured him that was the last thing I was doing — that I was lamenting the fact that his daughter and every other students' under-performance was not inherently reflective of their ability. The problem was the system in which the students were in, that were non-challenging and under-taught; but I assured him that all of those issues were being changed for the benefit of the students. This particular father stated, "My daughter has had straight A's since kindergarten and is a gifted 8th grader." I told him that, based on the District performance standards, his daughter had met the requirements for those marks and that designation but when compared nationally, his student was at or below the minimum requirements.

Some of the more disheartening statistics studied were that of student retention and matriculation.

Of the nearly 800 students in middle school, over 250 of them were over-age students (i.e. ages 16 -18 years old). **That's over 25%!**

While the statistics appeared to be better in high school (out of 1,200 students, approximately 150 (or approximately 15%) were over-age students (i.e. ages 19 – 20 years old), the reason the numbers were lower for high school students was because, the "young adults" simply dropped out of school and were no longer considered as part of the student population. The law stated that anyone 18 and over was allowed to cease attending school. Most of these young adults chose to pursue full-time employment instead of repeating 8th grade, *again*. Shockingly, the over-age students were the very students who attended school *every day*.

Punishment as a demotivating factor is something I will talk more about later, but for this particular point, let it suffice to say that suspension was the teachers' punishment of choice in secondary schools (middle and high schools). Here's why: suspension caused a student to fall behind in school work and attendance requirements for graduation; falling behind caused students' grades to drop; poor grades led to poor self-confidence; poor self-confidence axiomatically caused their grades to fall further.

Additionally, in elementary school, teachers recommended retaining students *excessively*. Instead of personalizing instruction for the students, teachers created macro lesson plans for classes in which their teaching method became the primary focus as opposed to student learning outcomes. Despite how bad the method of instruction was deemed, if the student did not learn or keep up with the pace of instruction, those students failed in elementary school and hence were "retained" to repeat the grade to get up to "standard" which contributed greatly to the over-age issues in the District.

Still, like so many other districts, the problem of over-age students and dropout rates was a generational problem. These generational curses of academic failure were enhanced by segregation and racial prejudices that are prevalent in the deep south and in particular in largely minority communities. For me, this was something foreign, I grew up in a home with a traditional nuclear family that included my siblings and a mom and dad. We lived in a neighborhood in Kansas City, Missouri that was rich with diversity and the school in which I had attended promoted the education and success of future citizens as opposed to perceived social limitations. I had, for the most part, been spared the pains of direct racial disparity. (Remember, my first real encounter with racial bias was thrown at me only a few months prior to standing in front of these Mississippians trying to convince them that their children were worth our best efforts, when I had essentially been fired from a job that I had just been offered—all based on the color of my skin, and the perceived beliefs and affiliations attributed to the color of my skin). The point I want to make is that even though the intellectual part of my brain realized what was happening, the emotional part of my brain did not *want* to believe it. As an educator, I sure was not ready to accept it! These students were being relegated to lower-class citizens and intellectual abilities simply because they had melanin in their skin. This was sickening and hard to really address without accepting that things had not changed all that much in the deep south. *But how can these people that employed me, a black man, still be consciously racist towards me and the students?* It was really a hard dichotomy to digest but it was a reality in which I lived.

More results came pouring in to explain some to the attitudes and resistance I was experiencing.

What I learned was that:

- The quality of principals and teachers were comparable to the economic condition of most of the students — poverty level or below.

- Nepotism and inappropriate relationships were rampant in the District. I literally got dizzy trying to keep it all straight (e.g. whom was related to whom; whom was messing with whom; and who was making money from what).

Walking into school board meetings or one of the District schools was like walking into a badly-scripted soap opera. No, it was more like walking into the parody of a *really* bad soap opera. I remember more than a few times when I was talking to friends and other school administrators about my situation — either to get advice or some much-needed moral support. They would often say things like, *"Are you serious?" "Are you sure you did not misunderstand?"* or *"There's no way they can do that."*

My response was always something to the effect of, *"You can't make this stuff up."*

More facts came pouring in:

The school board — the very people elected to protect and serve the students in our district — were as disengaged as one could imagine. A board member with school-aged children would not even consider sending them to the public schools because they knew the abysmal state in which they were found. Every District board member who had school-aged children sent their children to private schools where they could get a better education and be disassociated with those "poor black kids" in town. Indeed, in one of my first meetings, a board member said they would never send their children to these "black" schools.

Side note: The prejudices of the south were still very much alive. Segregation was the name of the game. Students continued to experience the discriminatory effects of institutional racism and unwritten Jim Crow attitudes. The students (mostly black students) were set up to fail before they ever entered the game.

I will use the example of travel to one of the most beautiful places in the world (or so I am told). While I have never been to Jamaica, everyone I know who has been there says the chasm between those who have and those who have-not is wide and deep. Those who have, have a whole lot. Those who do not have, have a whole lot of nothing. That's how it was (and still is) in "Nameless" Mississippi.

During one of the countless discussions regarding District funds, I was told (with absolute and unabashed candor) that the "school system" (which was code for poor kids) did not *deserve* the tax money that was apportioned to them. Even at that early stage in my time there, I was almost afraid to ask why they (most of the board members and other affluent members of the community) felt that way. However, I had to know for sure, because maybe— just maybe—if I knew why things were the way they were, I might have a better chance at fixing them. Or at the very least, working around and in spite of them. However, nothing could have prepared me for the answer I received. One board member stated that "the school system [the poor kids] does not need to reap the benefit of taxpayer money because most of their parents do not pay any taxes." Note that the racial code was always in the form of "taxpayers" (i.e. whites) and "non-taxpayers" (i.e. blacks).

"What?" was my perplexed reply. The board members continued that "most of the parents whose kids go to school are not taxpayers. They either do not make enough money to pay taxes, or they're on government assistance, so their income *is* tax money. So, if they do not contribute by paying taxes, they should not get the benefit of those taxes."

I could not believe what I was hearing. I simply could not believe that people today could be so socially and morally irresponsible and irreproachable. I tried to reason with them, I tried to explain that even though many of our parents paid little or no taxes when filing their income tax returns, they still paid taxes. They paid taxes on the food they purchased, the gas they consumed, the clothing they bought, and the utilities they used. Some paid property taxes that included school zoning taxes. These people also contributed to the tax base by providing expendable income to their landlords, as well as everywhere else they spent money. Besides, I said, "When did it become okay to punish people for being poor? When did it become acceptable to punish a child for their socio-economic situation?"

Just so we are clear, the resounding answer to those two questions should have been and should always be: NEVER. However, as I had soon learned, these folks had gotten away with doing things their discriminatory way for so long and without any form of accountability or retribution whatsoever that they could not even fathom the idea that someone might call them out for their discriminatory attitudes and unlawful racial biases. These people elected to power were so used to taking whatever they wanted, whenever they wanted, and from whomever they wanted that they felt they were entitled to the things they took no matter the discriminatory means to get it. They loathed and feared anyone who challenged them and set out to discredit and punish anyone who challenged them. But I was not afraid to put a stop to it… or at least try.

Chapter 4
Second on The Agenda...

I could almost feel the clock ticking away. Each day, students walked through the doors of the school and into classrooms, where teachers cared more about themselves, their social lives, and their relationships with other staff members (many of them inappropriate). Consequently, the kids were sinking away from their destination of a brightly educated future.

Teacher-related issues were not the only reason we were failing our students miserably. The district lacked essential programs and personnel; namely a special education director, a human resources director, public relations (PR) specialist and other leadership positions. We also lacked a curriculum that met State requirements and served to teach and equip our students for both their short-range and long-range futures.

After putting together a proposal for a suitable curriculum, I asked the board to adopt the curriculum into the school's education plan (such as it was). It took a few months for them to finally sign off on it — not because of funding, not because of flaws in the plan, but because they felt the need to make sure I knew they were the ones running the show and that I was not welcome in *"No Name"* Mississippi. The hostile environment was evident. What I did not know until I had been there for a while was the reason behind it. After all, they had offered me the job. I did not beg for it. So, why was there so much hate and animosity from day one? I am just as human as the next guy, so I wanted to be able to work with the board and the leadership team to the benefit of the students. I had left a perfectly good job where I was liked and respected. I had also uprooted my children and dropped them into failing schools, so making students THE priority and doing it with excellence was not just a professional goal. It was a personal one, too.

My first inclination was to "clean house". Start fresh. I soon found out, however, that replacing principals and teachers was not a viable option. Why? Because no one of the caliber I was seeking wanted to be a part of such a District with such a *Peyton Place* mentality. This was also the first time I understood the importance of a PR person to help control the narrative being created by local media that was controlled by the affluent in the community. Since firing my way out of the situation was not an option, I had to remedy the issues utilizing the staff already in place. I was fine with that, as long as they were willing to comply with the teaching and accountability standards that were put in place. Some were... others were not. But *everyone* had a lot of changing to do.

The culture of our buildings had to change because I was not about to let *their* main thing stay the main thing. No way! Students were my main thing and it was going to become their main thing, too. But change is hard and if done too quickly, leads to resistance. I had given a few hard mandates. My mantra was that we would never put the needs of adults over the needs of children. This was not an easy task for some of the staff, as they had created a culture where they had made themselves comfortable at the expense of the students.

To get things rolling in that direction, I let them know that their *family* mentality was no longer acceptable. We were not a family. We were a *team*.

Side note: Here's the difference between a family and a team: Families come together and accept each other, no matter the circumstances. Families overlook each other's flaws. Sometimes, they even step in to fill in the gaps, so these flaws will not negatively affect their loved one's life. Families have unconditional love for one another, and always protect each other.

A team, on the other hand, works to bring out the best in one another. They expect their teammates to play by the rules, to put their best foot forward, and to expend their talents and efforts for the good of the whole team. Team members who do this well are rewarded and recognized for their efforts and talents. Team members who do not participate according to the rules and ethics guidelines get "benched" and are expected to work harder to bring their skills up to par so they can play well enough to be an asset rather than a detriment. Members of a team do not have to love one another. They do not even have to like one another. But they *do* have to respect one another and work together. This was difficult (at best) for my staff to grasp. They were so entwined in each other's lives outside and inside the school that they could not, nor would they, draw the necessary lines between personal interaction and professionalism.

With that understanding, let us get back to the family versus team issues I was experiencing. Principals unashamedly admitted they did not give accurate evaluations of their teachers because they did not want to hurt their feelings or upset them. Familial or sexual relationships were often involved so they were not about to risk making their lover or their in-laws mad at them for saying anything negative about the way their partners did their job.

Several staff members also had the same sense of entitlement of the board members. The staff members believed that they deserved their jobs "just because" and that their students were just there "taking up space". Some of them honestly believed it was their *right* to spend their days at school doing whatever they felt like doing. It killed me to walk into the buildings and see how miserably we were failing our students! We were nothing more than an employment agency — hiring people out of formality. I cannot lie, it was a bit overwhelming. But on the other hand, it was also very motivating. My former boss was right in saying I was a hands-on kind of leader, I just never realized how much so until I got in the trenches in this role. I did not lead from my desk and many remarked that they had never seen any superintendent visit a school before. I was still very much interested and driven to be involved in the process rather than simply overseeing it.

Because of this, I wanted to inspire my teachers so that they also wanted to be part of the process. I wanted them to *want* to be better for themselves, as well as for our students. So, here's what I did: Armed with the data that the dropout rate among high school students was over 60% and the overall student performance level across all demographics decreased each year, I had an individual meeting with each principal and asked them separately the following question:

"If you had a student who scored 30% on a test, what grade would you give them?" Their answer was always quick and decisive. They would give them an F. I then asked, "if you had a teacher with a rating of 30%, would you keep them?" Obviously, the principals replied with "no". Next, I asked, "If you had a salesperson that sold 30% of your products, would you keep them?" The response was again, "No".

I pointed out that I had just described their job performance and asked why they felt they should still be employed. I then pointed out to them that this was exactly the grade they would allocate to students is the same grade that they deserved as an educator — an F. I explained that 30% (or lower) was the percentage of students they were adequately educating and preparing at their school building. But I did not stop there. I let them know I was there with them and desired that they perform at a passing rate and for them to do better — to be better leaders. I also made it abundantly clear that I did not expect them to do it on their own and that I would be there to help them with resources and assistance. I remember that after one of these discussions, one of our principals ran out crying and hyperventilating; I was taken aback and began to search for the principal when they did not return. I found her locked in the office with the assistant superintendent.

I asked what had happened and she explained that no one had ever told her she was a failure. I found out that several of the principals did not hear anything beyond, *"You deserve an F."* All they heard was that they needed to either shape up or ship out, and that the current status quo was no longer going to be the status quo. It was no longer going to be okay for janitors to have sex with kitchen workers or teachers *in the building* or *while school was in session.* They totally missed the support I had offered and the goal of getting our students to perform at or above the State of Mississippi minimum requirements.

In addition, I also attempted to make radical changes in our athletic program. The basketball coach, who had been there for over 30 years, was the most predictable coach ever. He had not changed his play book once in all the years he had been there, so generations (literally) knew every move his team was going to make, every. single. time. So, even though this school district is the oldest school district in the entire state of Mississippi, and he was the most tenured coach in the State, we had never won a State Championship of any kind… in any sport. I could not believe it — especially since the first year I was there, our basketball team consisted of a few juniors that were 6'9" and we were boasting an individual freshman that had just won an Olympic Gold medal.

But there they were, playing the same ole game and losing. Our kids and our community deserved better, so I fired him. It was not a popular decision. I was almost at the end of my first semester there, and already knew that no decision I made would be popular. Nonetheless, I was not there to be popular or to be welcomed into *their* family. I was there to create a school district in which the students came first. Always. Now, here's the really irritating thing — everyone wanted him to go. They wanted a winning team, but since *"He's such a nice guy,"* and he had been *their* coach and their dad's coach before that, they were reluctant to let him go.

One important, prominent black doctor said, "He was a great moral compass for the boys, so do we really need to fire him?" This was that family mentality that I was trying to change, the mentality that was detrimental to the progress of the District and the student's welfare. I was up against this stagnant mentality. But, I held my ground, and hired a new coach — a coach that led us to the District's *first* state championship in the history of the District. The win naturally generated a lot of excitement, but even that only lasted for so long. Other than the coach, despite what the media and others said, I did not fire anyone else. Several teachers **quit** because they saw the proverbial "handwriting on the wall", but I did not fire them. I had even explained that the possibility of me terminating a teacher's employment was impossible since I was not authorized to terminate a teachers' employment with the District.

I was not there every day to observe them. My job was to hold their principal accountable, which held the teachers accountable.

However, in the principals' cases, I tried to transition them into other positions, but even that came with some backlash. For example, a principal in one of our schools announced that for Black History month, they would be holding a cookout and serving traditionally "southern foods". I thought it was a great idea; one that showed initiative towards making learning more fun and interactive for the students. So, on the day of said cookout, two of my assistants and I went to observe and to participate.

Prior to leaving the office to go to that particular school, I received a couple of phone calls from the municipal utilities stating that the electricity in that particular building (and surrounding areas) were having issues in that the electricity was going off and on. Well, we rushed to the scene where we discovered the hallways were lined with tables filled with boilers, cookers, and crockpots plugged into *every* outlet. The building reeked of all sorts of food smells (most of which were unpleasant). I was told that the menu consisted of food that *"slaves would have eaten"* and *"every part of a pig."* They had persevered through several power outages and kept cooking. My attitude quickly changed when I realized that there were no students in the hallways — or anywhere else for that matter — participating in this cookout.

In fact, every single classroom had a substitute teacher that day. The only ones in the hallway for the so-called "cookout" were the teachers! They were having their own little party that had nothing to do with student advancement or education about or experiencing *black history*. This event could have been done after school or on the weekend, during their free time, but that was inconvenient for them. I radioed for the principal, but I encountered the assistant principal. When I asked what was going on, I was informed (in no uncertain terms) that she did not have to talk to or answer to *"a little boy"* (meaning me). Biting my tongue and swallowing my anger, I found the principal. When I told the principal that I needed to have a word with her, she informed me that any conversations we had would need to include her husband and that she did not appreciate me telling her she was doing her job inappropriately. I pulled her aside away from the staff and said she was supposed to be the leader of this school and she was undermining her own authority by stating that her husband needed to be here to talk for her. It was something I had never experienced with a professional staff—I had never encountered someone requesting their spouse (not a member of management) to be present in a discussion with their place of employment.

As you can see, even leadership was in short supply as I attempted to build this organization. After that day, I started making regular pop-in visits to the school and documenting everything I observed and heard. Not long after that, both the principal and the assistant principal resigned.

Now here's where the situation got sad, yet somewhat comical. After receiving the principal's resignation, I moved her to a different position. This woman was actually a very nice person and very personable with students, so I did not want to lose her altogether. But when I made the transition effective, her husband started calling me. He said I was out of line for harassing and picking on her. He even asked, yes, *he* asked if she could keep her principal's salary in the new (lower) position. Of course, I said no, which did not sit very well with her or her husband. Furthermore, because this former principal's husband was a respected influencer in the community, I started getting threats over this whole ordeal, too. That's right — I said 'too' because even though I was not even a year into the job, I was already receiving physical threats on an almost-daily basis.

Chapter 5
When the Truth Is Ugly

I am a focused and disciplined man. I have worked in every position in education. I have five graduate degrees in addition to a doctorate. I worked my way up the administrative ladder and worked hard to be successful for my community. So, when I received a call from the *"No Name"* Mississippi school district offering me the job of superintendent of schools where 90% of the student population is black, I admit, part of me wondered if ethnicity and the color of my skin had something to do with their decision. After all, we are talking about Mississippi — a southern state that is widely known for the murder of Emmett Till (a 14-year old African-American male that was abducted and brutally murdered by two white men based on an unwarranted lie told by a white woman), a southern state that is known for its segregated high school dances in the 21st century, and a southern state which is still inundated with racial prejudices that are painfully obvious.

(Okay, so that's not quite fair. Not everyone feels this way. Not everyone in this beautiful State is still carrying chips on their shoulders against people of color. Not everyone considers black people — especially poor black children — a disposable commodity. Not everyone saw me as a troublemaker out to prove I had risen above their generations-old boundaries. But from day one in that particular part of Mississippi, I found myself in a hostile and toxic environment.)

The question was why. Why did the school board choose me then *fight* against me on every suggestion and recommendation I made?

Why, when I applied for (and was awarded) 100% free lunches school-wide, were the parents and students outraged? I got an answer to this question soon after I had announced the award. It was a hate/pride-related issue. The families that sent their children to the District did not want to be viewed as being eager to take handouts or charity. Yes, these people were impoverished but they were not lazy, most of them worked to provide food for their families so *they* were not the ones with the problem of entitlement; it was the board and the stigma of what accepting the federal award of lunch subsidy would mean.

Still, when I presented the free lunch status, I also explained how it was an asset to children's education (i.e. kids who are nutritionally fit and have a "full belly" are better able to focus in class and retain what they learn). The families were more receptive, or maybe the better word to use would be "accepting" of this benefit. However, soon after the federal government approved our program, there was a marked difference in attitudes and I, personally, was amazed to see the difference.

Many children started to bring their lunch from home. Many of the Caucasian children and even some working-class families of African-American children did the same. When I asked the students for the reason, some of them stated that they did not want "government handouts". No matter what I said or did, city officials informed me the federal subsidy was *not* going to happen. You read that correctly, not school board members, but rather *city* officials, who crossed their jurisdictional authority to invade mine.

Old money business owners were problematic too. I naturally asked myself why these people thought I answered to them. Even more perplexing, though, was how they knew everything that was internally confidential.

Actually, it was not all that hard to figure out. There was obviously a 'leak' or two... or perhaps three in the office and/or board. I hardly had time to take a breath before this person (or people) ran straight to a very influential man in town who "just happened" to own both the local newspaper and the television station. How convenient, right? (Remember, I mentioned that the local media was controlled by influence, not by standards or ethics in First Amendment-style journalism).

It would have been one thing if these leaks would have been truthful and accurate, but truth and accuracy were not in their vocabularies. One of the first experiences I had with this was their misinformation (lies) regarding the amount of money the District had received in selling the textbooks back to the company from which they were purchased. They skewed the incident to make it look as if one of my first acts as superintendent was to cost the district thousands of dollars by refusing to use the textbooks and insist on tablets that could not possibly be as flexible and beneficial as I had claimed. They were not even willing to concede on the issue after it made national news with several *respected* online magazines highlighted our district for being innovative forerunners for choosing tablets over *physical* textbooks. I wish I could say that was the worst of it, but it was not. Character assassination and lodging threats was their specialty. I had not been there too terribly long before a news reporter offered herself to me sexually, which by the way I turned down without hesitation. These people were out to destroy both my personal and professional character, and I soon found out there were no boundaries they would not cross.

Another "round" started when I had to release the championship basketball coach for issues I will just call "highly justifiable" and ask you to trust me on that. This decision really upset the entire town, so it came as no surprise to me when I got a visit from the community's top leader. He told me I needed to rehire the coach or that my reputation and character would be destroyed — that they could spread rumors from which I would never recover. I stood my ground and did not rehire the coach; and sure enough, as was promised, later that day fake emails were sent around, claiming that I was gay and had a gay lover.

Following that came a phone call saying that if I did not pay $4,000 to the caller, the newspaper was going to make every effort to take the rumor nation-wide and spread it on the internet. I told them extortion and fear did not change the truth and that I was standing by my decision to terminate the coach. Unsurprisingly, before long, my name was everywhere. I must admit that these rumors and false allegations were hurtful and *very* exhausting. I had come there to try to heal a sick and dying school district with confidence that I could do so, but the *process and the progress* was painfully slow because of the non-stop drama in which I found myself on a daily basis.

But by the grace of God (and my momma's voice constantly whispering in my ear), I managed to hold my head high and focus on what I had been hired to do. Every time I was tempted to retaliate or lower myself to their level, I heard my momma's voice whispering in my ear reminding me, as she always did when I was a kid, *"God says a good name is better than silver or gold."* I knew she was right — she usually is — so I did not sink down to their level. I told myself repeatedly every single day that their pettiness and hatred were not worth disappointing my momma or not being true to myself. Besides, there were a lot bigger and tougher battles that needed to be fought and won than denying some small-town rumor or giving in to an extortion scheme.

Money — that was a huge issue in the district. When I say it was an issue, I do not mean there was a lack of it. I mean that it was being grossly mishandled, misused, and out and out illegally distributed. The first red flag that went up on this problem was when I was not 'allowed' access to certain financial records. I did not let that stop me from taking charge of things, though, and as you will read later on, during my time as superintendent of that district, we had a balanced budget every year.

For the first time in 10 years, the district did not have a shortfall. We did not have to borrow money from the city to pay the bills. Not only that, but there were significant construction improvements at the same time, including the construction of a sports facility as well as a technological overhaul. But like I said — more on that later. For now, I wanted to set the stage for what I was working against.

*A few years prior to my arrival, a board proposal had been passed to build a new school facility. The board reported the building costs to be much higher than they were, and many skimmed the 'fat' off and kept it for themselves.

*There was a staff person in my office who acted as a Director for the District. Her salary was $80,000 a year. If she was benefitting the district through her efforts, then yes, she would definitely be considered an asset. This staff person, however, had NEVER EVER performed the functions of her job description. But what I found out was that she was "best friends" with the mayor, who, by the way, was one of the top naysayers in this whole ordeal. Because of their relationship, this employee was supposedly untouchable in regard to rerouting her to a position in which she was more suited. She appeared nice, friendly (in an appropriate way), and certainly deserved to be given a chance to prove herself. But remember — I was not there to be part of their family—I was there to develop a team of staff members that would assist with the realignment of District policies and infrastructure for the benefit of the students.

So, when I engaged in an evaluation of her particular performance as dictated by the job description and presented her with the facts regarding her job performance, I did so with the intention of either coaching her into acceptable performance or putting her in a different mindset to pursue different opportunities. I should not have been surprised when (instead of seeing it as constructive criticism and accountability) she took it as an attack on a personal and professional level. She resigned the next day but put the word out in the community that she had been unjustly fired. Her attitude drastically changed from welcoming me into my new position upon my arrival to doing one of the pettiest acts I have ever witnessed. Let me explain: as part of making me feel welcome in my new office, this person had equipped my office bathroom with a new toilet seat and urinal mat. But after I had made the decision to reroute her based on her subpar performance, she came to the office while I was out for a while to demand the toilet seat and used urinal mat back from my secretary. My secretary gave her the items she requested. What I found out is that this person literally hauled these things out of the office only to take them to the nearest Goodwill store to donate them—yes, perfectly functioning District-purchased items were donated without approval to a local Goodwill store out of spite because the individual had been re-routed to another position.

*Tax money... *tax money* that was legally required to be used by the schools for the schools was being re-distributed by the board and spent on and for the private schools that the board member's children were attending. Take a minute to let that soak in. The board took money from the public-school fund and funneled those into the *private* schools of which their children attended. Again... let that soak in so you can get a mental picture of what was going on. The members of the school board would not send their children to the public schools they were supposedly directing and supporting because they did not want their children's education to suffer at the hands of teachers who were inadequately trained, inadequately supervised, and inadequately equipped. Furthermore, they also did not *want* their children to "have to" go to school with all the poor kids (black or white).

*Money budgeted for the Music Department (for instruments and the like) was not made accessible to the Music Department. I naturally wanted to know why. Did they not need it? I decided to check the situation out — just to make sure. When I did, I discovered students were playing on worn-out, broken-down instruments. I kid you not — more than a few of them were being held together by duct tape. You read that correctly — duct tape! I wasted no time gathering these so-called instruments. I took them to the board meeting and said I thought now would be a good time to get the kids some new instruments. There was nothing they could say or do to skirt that issue, so the kids received their instruments.

*In just about any small or mid-sized town in the US, Friday night high school sports are a big deal — especially football in a lot of cases. But let me tell you, in *"No Name"* Mississippi, high school football was not just big — It was huge! It was mega-huge! These people lived for Friday night football (and basketball, too). And I was right in there with them. I had played football in high school back in KC and at Mizzou during my early college career. My oldest son, who was in high school, was also a linebacker for the team. So, you bet I was in the stands cheering them on as loud and proud as anyone else. But the school board and big-Whigs of the community could not even leave something as special and "sacred" as high school football alone. You know how anywhere else you would go, the parents of the football team, cheerleaders, and band kids are the ones who would collect the money for the tickets? And how these same folks or students in the FFA, Honor

Society, or Spanish Club would be working the concession stands? Not here. The school board members and their community cohorts were the ones taking the money — money my office did not see for days (sometimes up to a week) until after the event. When I finally saw the figures on the receipts, it did not take long for me to figure out something was not right.

The amount of money reported could not possibly be correct considering the number of people paying to get in and enjoying concessions while they were there. I was not about to accuse anyone of anything. That would not have accomplished anything aside from more threats and attacks on me and my family. Instead, I just issued a directive that District staff would collect the money on game nights from the ticket booth and from the concession stands. Miraculously, revenues increased dramatically. Unfortunately, so did the threats against me, and the false media reports.

*One of the first things I asked for when I came to the District — aside from the curriculum and the tablets instead of textbooks — was for a director of special education and a human resources director. The school board out and out refused the human resources position. For a while, I did not get it — I could not find anything to indicate why they were so reluctant to do that. But then one night, I happened to be in the office much later than usual when a woman came into the building. I knew she was not on staff, but I thought maybe she was a night janitor I just did not recognize. No such "luck". I found out that she was the secretary to the human resources director in a neighboring school district who was being paid *under the table* to sneak in at night and "do" human resource work for us! I had no idea that such shenanigans were happening right under my nose because there was certainly no evidence of her "work". Yet another misappropriation of funds by the board that I was now required to investigate. In fact, unbeknownst to me, the District was cited by the State before I arrived for allowing unauthorized personnel to access private and confidential information. I also found out that this was how confidential hiring decisions were already given to politicians and public news outlets. It was all too much at one point.

*Let's recap the obstacles that plagued my leadership: inept teachers who were capable of doing much more than the performance they were exhibiting; a board that did not care about anyone but themselves; false rumors created against me; racial prejudices against me, extortion, frustration at not being able to control me, and illegal mob-like activity made for a pretty full plate. These things paled in comparison, though, to the hateful and life-threatening actions against me. Sometimes, I actually stopped and asked myself if I had stepped through some sort of time machine without realizing it and had landed in the 1960s. I had not. I was just living in a community in which the "right" people had not made it to the twenty-first century.

Another example, and indeed one of the most disturbing revelations about the local media in this city, was how information was controlled and manipulated. I should have picked up on that right away when some of the first words I heard upon my arrival in town was a warning to *not* read the newspaper. I soon realized why I was given the warning. It was because the paper abused its First Amendment powers with lack of journalistic integrity and dishonest persuasion of the community against the District. I also realized why the board refused to allow me to hire a Director of PR. This person would have naturally written content to inform the community on the positive changes the District was making and the successes that the District enjoyed because of those changes. That, however, would have been counter-productive to the newspaper's intent.

As it was, the local newspaper only printed negative things about the District. There was rarely anything positive reported, unless, of course, it was about the private schools in the community. Even when the District paid for advertisements and various editorial articles to be printed, the newspaper staff changed them. I even tried going the press release route. That is, from a journalistic viewpoint, the statements I submitted were to be printed as received. They were not. The newspaper would either omit parts of the official press release, print it out of context, or report that I had declined to comment on something that I was either not contacted about or that I had made positive comment and it was never printed. We, as in the trusted members of my staff, and I finally took another route and developed our own narrative. We built a platform and delivered the District's own news digitally.

We wanted our students and their parents to see how wonderful, smart and progressive the student body was becoming and to show the world how proud we were of their accomplishments. The problem was that they had limited access to technology and the newspaper took full advantage of that. A former employee of the paper later told me that he had personally called them out for taking the "anonymous tip" that I was gay and printing it as truth without any investigation into the claims. He also told me that they went to great lengths to control the ideas and thoughts of the people.

The situation felt a lot like wartime propaganda of which I was targeted as the "bad leader" they wanted to destroy. It was like living back in the days of McCarthy-ism, or like I was in a modern-day event similar to ones experienced by Anne Moody in her memoir *"Coming of Age in Mississippi."* In this book, Moody details her life growing up in the Jim Crow South and her role in the Civil Rights Movement. Although the attacks and threats against me pale in comparison to what Moody (and so many others) experienced, it was clear that the same hate, anger, and ignorance that led to oppression of the undereducated was still alive and well. Indeed, I felt like a purposeful headline introducing my life in Mississippi would have read, *"Dr. Hickman chronicles his administration under Jim Crow-style policies and the lynching mentality of the Deep South in his instructional leadership memoir."*

EXECUTION BY FIRING SQUAD

Chapter 6
The Fear Was Real

Up until now, this story, this true story has revolved around the obstacles I faced as a leader. I have revealed how personalities, misconceptions, greed, insecurity, and fear or resistance to change can cause people to resort to extreme measures to serve their own selfish needs and desires. As a result, these people inflict damage on innocent, voiceless victims — in this case, the students — with no remorse. When you think about it, it all boils down to two things: selfishness and fear.

The selfish part is easy to see. The fear, however, was masked as arrogance, pride, and entitlement. No matter what it looked like, though, it was fear. These people were afraid of change. Afraid of being exposed for who and what they really are. Afraid of someone (in this case, me) doing something more or better than they could. Afraid of admitting that their racial and socio-economic prejudices and hatred were wrong. Afraid of being dethroned and recognized for who and what they really are. Afraid of anything they could not control.

When a dog feels threatened, it bites. Sometimes, they even bite the one they love and trust the most. When a bee is in danger, it stings. When a snake feels it is in danger, it strikes. When a rooster believes its territory is being infringed upon, it attacks. When the board members and those controlling the community in that little piece of Mississippi felt threatened, they did all those things. Something else their fear did was to brood inside of others, and as the saying goes, *"fear breeds contempt"* and the contempt and hatred was real. Their contempt and hatred were directed towards me, which in turn caused me to be fearful.

The fear I felt was both real and justifiable. Still, today when I think about the verbal and physical threats made against me, part of me still shudders, while the other part of me gets angry. Did they not realize what they were doing? Did they not care? Did they really feel their actions were justified? Morally acceptable?

As you read the following pages, I need you to do so knowing why I am sharing these darkest of moments with you. It is to prove that quality leadership—even under fire—is possible; to encourage you to persevere in doing the right thing no matter what; to inspire you to always be your best self rather than sink to the level of depravity and corruption around you; and to remind you that when things like prejudice and hate are allowed to live in even a small "container" they wield forceful and deadly blows at their victims.

Finally, I am sharing these things because I need to be able to say these things out loud so that no one can rightly accuse me of keeping these things hidden because they are true. I have suffered greatly, both personally and professionally, because of these lies and I am ready for people to know that Dr. Phillip Hickman is not afraid, and it is time for me to rise. My silence has been a time of healing and recovery. But I am healed now and ready once more to lead teachers and students to their highest possible level of accomplishment and success.

I also need you to understand what my reasons for sharing these things are NOT. I know — it is not grammatically correct, but for the sake of making my point, it will have to do. I am not sharing these things with you for the purpose of slandering people. If that were so, I would be naming names. I am not sharing these things in order to stir up arguments or tension regarding racial issues. The color of a person's skin or the amount of money they have in the bank is of no concern to me. I am interested in what is inside a person — what truly makes them who they *are* and who they can become. I am not sharing these things to try to illicit pity or anything like that. I am not sharing these things for the purpose of fanning the flames of contention. Now, all that said, it is time to tell you a true story about a group of people in Mississippi that did their best to break me... as I have already stated, my arrival in town was met with a hostility that I did not understand. What I was told later, however, was that the Interim Superintendent, who had been filling the position until I was hired, was the wife of a local millionaire. She had basically been promised the position by some members on the school board after assuring her the salary package would be a hefty one.

What this board member did not count on, however, was after getting the salary package pushed through, the Interim Superintendent did not get the needed votes to secure the position. True or not, I do not know whether they put the job out there and then interviewed me to make it look like they were above-board or whether they wanted to consider their options. But what I do know now is that it was not supposed to turn out the way it did. The margin was narrow — 3/2 — so I just barely made it, but I did not look at it like that. With that small of a board, the chances of it being like that were pretty significant. I chose to take it as meaning I was going to have to put my best foot forward and show them what I was capable of as quickly as possible — which was what I intended to do since the students were "code blue" and needed help ASAP. I was not the only one intending to expeditiously handle business. The board, certain members of the community, and a significant number of teachers and other staff members did not waste any time in letting me know I was not welcomed and that they were going to make the four years of my contract a living hell...that is, if I lasted all four years. In fact, the board member that did not follow the plan was replaced for *not* voting against me. This had become a pattern as I only had a five-person board but seven different board members in four years, with only one particular board member remaining the entire four years which was deadest on creating a hostile work environment for me.

I have pretty much set the scene, so I am not going to go into a lot of details about specific events leading up to the threats made upon me. I am just going to give you a recap of some of the memorable "highlights" in order to help you understand just how bad things can get without you getting sucked into an abyss of depravity. So, without putting them in any real sequential order (or order of relevance and severity) take a look at a few of the "arrows" fired at the bullseye — which was me. *It is a wonder how I am still alive.*

For Sale

Early-on, I had to establish the habit of leaving the office in the middle of the afternoon to remove the numerous 'for sale' signs from our yard. This was not a one or two-time occurrence. It happened regularly. You would think they would have gotten tired of wasting time on something as juvenile as that, but they did not. The only reason I was so concerned about it was because I did not want my kids to come home and find them there — or to read some of the hateful slurs written on them. They were trying to settle in and start over in a new house, new community, new environment, new everything and make new friends. They did not need to have doubts planted in their minds about whether we were staying or about our safety.

Bribe and Prejudice

Board members regularly approached my staff members trying to bribe them to file sexual and racial harassment suits and other types of complaints against me.

Some even offered sexual "favors" in exchange for teachers and administrators keeping their jobs. I must remind you that I was a married man with a family. These bribes and set-ups were designed to ruin my family and my career.

Death Threats

I received threatening "anonymous" phone calls regularly regarding my personal safety. They would tell me that they were coming to my office or house to get me. I would respond that "they better come to my job and catch me in my suit because I will protect my home".

To try to reduce the stress level on my body, I made a concerted effort to exercise regularly. One day while I was out jogging, a truck started following me; driving as slowly as possible beside the sidewalk on which I was jogging. (My neighborhood was situated as such that you did not just wander into it or use it to pass through on your way to somewhere else. One was there because you needed to be there.) Anyway, this truck pulls up to me, rolls down the window, and asked if I was Philip Hickman, Superintendent of the schools. I stopped and just as I was about to answer, the man leaned over to pick something up. I could see in the mirror of the truck that he was picking up a rifle. I was terrified, but equally determined not to let him know it. So, I did something I had never done before and never will again. I denied my identity and said, "No sir, my name isn't Philip Hickman sir" (that too was stated in a southern "slave" voice). He asked again, "You are not Dr. Philip Hickman — the Superintendent of schools here in "No Name" Mississippi"? "No sir, I am not Dr. Hickman, sir," I repeated.

Then I turned away and started jogging again; trying to look as nonchalant as possible for a guy whose legs were pure rubber and whose heart was beating so hard it almost made my shirt move. I started to run in a zigzag fashion in case the person decided to start shooting (I had learned this from growing up in the city).

I kept up that pace until I was out of sight, although I could still see that man looking outside of his truck pointing a long object at me. After I was sure I was out of sight, I took off running as fast as I could. I ran through a wooded area that surrounded my home and came out the other side in a different neighborhood. I had no idea where I was in relationship to my house. I did not know if the streets would connect and take me home or not, and I knew I could not run back. Luckily there was a mail carrier running her route who told me she would be glad to give me a ride home. She said, *"I know you — you're my neighbor, you live just down the street from me and my family."* I can honestly say I had never been so glad in all my life to hear the word "neighbor".

After this incident, a particular board member and several staff members on my immediate team (there were several) came to me various times warning me of plots against me or to tell me they had been threatened or offered bribes to "turn" on me. I even had several staff members who started suffering from extreme anxiety due to the pressure for them to act in illegal and unethical ways.

After the more serious threats made against me, I decided to apply for a conceal and carry license in the state. I had a license in other states in which I had lived, but just had not taken the time to apply for one in Mississippi. However, be assured that I never took the gun onto school property, although I did keep a gun in my car.

But when some of my adversaries found out that I had obtained the permit, Batman-like rumors were circulated depicting me walking around the town with my suit jacket flopping open to show my "piece". Apparently, these allegations were meant to depict me in a dangerous light because I was supposedly "strapped" with an assortment of weapons. Immediately, those same people started plotting a plan to frame me for having a gun on school property. Thankfully, one of my trustworthy staff members got wind of it and warned me, and we were able to stop them from pursuing a frivolous arrest.

Confirmation

Towards the end of my four years in the District, I was in the 24-hour gym around 1:00 AM working out. One day (still trying to manage the stress through exercise), a member of the County Sheriff's office greeted me. After returning the greeting, he moved closer to me and in a quieter tone of voice said, "I am glad to see you're still here". Thinking he was referring to the fact that I had not let the school board run me out of town, I replied by saying something to the effect that I was there for the students and that until my contract was completed, I was not going anywhere. He looked at me with a concerned look on his face and then said, "No, that's not what I mean. I mean I am glad you're still here... still alive".

It was my turn to give him the perplexed look. He went on to tell me that someone at "the top" had put a bounty on my head payable to anyone who "got rid of me" (that is to say "to kill me"). This particular guy had been on the local police force at the time and had the guts to speak up in opposition of this plot to murder me, encouraging them to think about my family. His "defiance" cost him backlash on the force. I knew he had switched jobs, but I just had no idea why. He assured me he was not upset about that. He was happier being a county officer, he said, and happy that no one had taken the "bait".

Curiosity got the best of me, so I asked why he thought no one took the offer. He did not hesitate a minute to tell me that it was because despite what the power players in town said and how they felt, the parents and regular joes in town had a great deal of respect for me and actually liked me. They knew I was in their corner fighting for their kids, and they were grateful for it. He also mentioned that the town had just had a similar situation to Michael Brown, where an officer shot and killed an unarmed man, and they had too many people observing their actions. Knowing someone hated you so much that they wanted you dead is not something you just shake off, though. It cut deep and made me suspicious of nearly everyone around me. After that, I spent a lot more time looking over my shoulder than anyone should ever have to experience.

Family Attack

My oldest son also endured the brunt of some of their hatred towards me. My son carried a 4.0 GPA and had been the starting linebacker on the team since his sophomore year. He was amongst the best members they had on the football team. I am not saying that because I am his dad, I am saying that because it is what everyone said and because it is what the stats showed. But because he was my son, the coaches began to bench him from the "starting" position. They purposely tried to negate his ability to record "starting player" on his college and scholarship applications.

These coaches would put him on the field in rotation as opposed to starting him on plays. I knew it bothered him. I knew I could not say anything, though, because I would have instantly been labeled as a bully and accused of extracting favors from my staff in an unethical manner.

I will be forever proud and grateful to my son for his maturity, endurance and understanding during this tumultuous time. He was not blind or deaf to the circumstances and heard everything that was going on and how I was being targeted. He took it all in stride and did his Dad proud by doing his best with the circumstances forced upon him.

There was, however, a time when I did step in — not as the Superintendent, but as a parent. I made this very clear to his teacher when I requested to meet with her. She was giving him a near-failing grade in a class that was elective and meant to be more self-driven than academic. He had all A's and attended college classes where he attained A's as well. The only exception was this *one* high school elective class. I could not believe that he was almost failing a class that was right in the crux of his long suit abilities. There was no way he was doing that badly in that class. In fact, the purpose of the class was to ease his more extracting load because along with his high school classes, he was taking a full load of college classes as well. When I pressed the matter, she admitted she was biased against him because of a "beef" another teacher had with me and that she had given him a poor grade as a result (even though he deserved much better). She admitted it after she had recorded zero for his work but forgot to empty the trash before I came. I saw all of his work in the wastebasket and used that to get her to admit her wrongdoings.

Staff Misconduct

About mid-way through my time there, I started hearing rumors about a few of the teachers having sex (and other forms of inappropriate contact) with students. I immediately called the authorities, who... are you ready for this... admitted they knew there were things going on that should not be, but that they did not want to embarrass the teachers or bring "bad press" to the community. They also did not want to ruin the teachers' reputations, so they informed me I needed to stay out of it and let them do their job the way they felt it should be done.

I was beyond outraged! I was more than outraged! But I also knew that if I did not handle the situation carefully, I would end up making things worse than they already were for these kids. Nonetheless, I also could not just sit back and pretend nothing was wrong, so I made sure these kids knew I was on their side and that I would do whatever I could to protect them.

The authorities handled the investigation in silence, but they took the word of the adults over the students. To avoid further controversy, the authorities allowed the teachers to resign with no further investigation or charges. Instead, these same individuals were allowed to go work in *another* district. I felt helpless and indeed was rendered powerless to do anything about these egregious behavioral conduct violations.

False and Misleading

Shortly after I was hired, someone (supposedly from my past) sent an email to a board member "reporting" that I was a convicted rapist, that I have other felonious convictions, and that I had a "fake" resume.

First of all, had any of these allegations been even remotely true, they, along with every District I ever worked for would have found this information during my background check during the hiring process. Secondly, with social media and other online resources openly available to find out anything you want to know (and then some) about anyone, this information would have surfaced during the hiring process. Normally, I would have ignored such juvenile and unfounded fabrications; but due to the nature of these allegations and because these accusations were so severe, I was not going to just let this one drop. I started an investigation that included tracing the origination of the email. The origin of that email left me speechless. Would you like to know where it came from? One of the board members' *personal* business office.

Media Blitz

As some of you might have read, I was accused by the media of stealing more than $21,000 from the schools. The fact that this was an outright lie without one shred or ounce of evidence presented against me was more evidence against the lack of the journalistic integrity that should have been the backbone of the local media. They never printed that it was impossible for me to misuse or steal anything from the schools as the budget office was solely responsible for reviewing and examining expenditures that were approved by the school board. Still, these facts did not stop the newspaper from printing these false and misleading statements.

Ultimately, it was discovered that a board member was feeding the newspaper all the false information and making up slanderous stories about me and the District.

Slashers

Unfortunately, I spent a lot of money on tires because for some reason or another, they were magnets to "nails" and other sharp objects. One time, while traveling two hours away from home to make a presentation at a State meeting of educators, I had a blowout because of a "nail" peculiarly placed in my tire. On that trip, the brakes also seemed "off". Since this was my official car — the car provided to me by the District—for District-related business, I was never responsible for maintenance. Keeping in line with school policy, I found out that the vo-tech class at the high school were responsible for inspecting the vehicle. The vo-tech said it was fine.

However, the answer seemed "off". In fact, the idea that the superintendent's car was being repaired and serviced by unlicensed and uncertified vo-tech students was suspicious. So, I secretly took it (at *my* expense) to an auto mechanic in town. It took the mechanic only a few minutes to discover that tampering was evident with my vehicle. I paid for the repairs and left with yet another reason to keep one eye open at all times.

Unwelcomed and Unwanted

The lowest of lows (even lower than nearly having a gun pulled on me, or knowing my car had been tampered with, or hearing that there was a price on my life) was the fact that the people in the community despised me so much that they even had hatred on a day of mourning. Ironically, the car tampering incident happened on the day I attended the funeral of a staff member.

I went to the funeral home and made my way through the receiving line like everyone else did. In this small community, I made it my priority to attend the funerals of any staff or students (unfortunately, for this small community there were many funerals). But this particular time, things were different. When it was my turn, I greeted the family with my sincerest sympathies over their loss and expressed that their loss was also ours. I lamented that this particular teacher had been an asset to the students and to the District. Afterwards, I made my way towards the back of the chapel to take a seat, wishing to save the more prominent seats for those who knew her intimately.

However, not long after I sat down, a large man approached me as I was sitting preparing for the service. This man was the boyfriend of the daughter of the deceased. He explained to me that the family had asked him to tell me that I was not welcome there and that he was there to escort me out of the funeral home. Of course, I left without incident or without requiring a group of men to physically remove me. I certainly did not want to cause a scene and I certainly did not want to be where I was not welcome.

But the pain and ache in my heart that day was complete and total agony. It was almost unbearable. Was their hatred so strong that they could not set it aside even when they were grieving? Were they really so hardened against an outsider— one who desperately wanted to be a part of their lives — that they would refuse the kindness and sympathy of someone who cared about *their* loved one? I remember vividly feeling worthless at that point. I admit that I drove home crying as I was simultaneously empathizing with the family and asking God how one can be hated that much. (Even now, there are really no words to express how sad I was, and still am, for the darkness of their spirits and their hearts).

Leadership Anxiety

By the time the second semester of my fourth year rolled around, I was battle-weary and dealing with what could easily be "diagnosed" as the PTSD of leadership. The trauma was not from the profession itself, but rather the environment in which I was operating.

Throughout the course of my time in Mississippi, I still maintained and gained a great deal of respect from my peers; made significant contributions to the field of education; and earned several prestigious awards and recognitions for my work and innovative methods in this particular school district. Being a part of various committees and boards was my lifeline. These accolades and opportunities, along with the students themselves, were the compasses that kept me on track. However, one particular meeting acted as the catalyst for my decision to finally say "enough is enough".

I had had all I could take, and a goldfish could have figured out my contract was not going to be renewed, but I was determined to not let them fire me for something that I did **not** do. I knew that I would also be looking for a new position at the end of my contract, so I did not want "fired" on my resume.

I had high accolades from the education community throughout the United States. I had never been fired from anything in my life. In fact, during my four years at this District in *"No Name"* Mississippi, I had never been counseled verbally; I had never been reprimanded; I had never been written up; I had not had any grievances filed against me; nor had I ever been placed on administrative leave. In fact, I had even received excellent job evaluations ***all four years***, with the last excellent evaluation given on January 26th, just a few days before they recommended to terminate me which was one day after I filed a grievance to the board. Although, in the world outside of education, I would have been considered a protected class against retaliation based on the grievance to my employer; I was fired two days later, even after received a stellar evaluation.

That's right, after a stellar evaluation and progressive advancements in the District, I was fired. You may be asking on what basis did they fire me? Well here is exactly the events that they claimed were "terminable" events:

I had traveled to California as a District representative to work with a top company in the U.S. to assist with their school improvement technology products and to consult on the aspects of technology and entrepreneurism. One evening, however, I purchased appetizers for myself and a group of people who were vendors at the event. Things like this were not part of the school stipend for the trip, so I paid for them using my own credit card. But the hotel inadvertently charged both my card and my District p-card for these appetizers. The value of the appetizers for the table was approximately $50. As soon as my secretary caught the mistake, she contacted the hotel to have it corrected asked them to make note of the fact that the error had been theirs. They gladly complied and even sent a note acknowledging their error to the District — along with the reimbursement.

No big deal, right? Wrong. I was fired over the incident. This was the final straw, they said. Final straw? For what? They had proof in black and white that it was an error on the part of the hotel and that the $50 was back in the District's account. But their level of harassment and retaliation led them to give me a letter of termination for $50. A $50 error, that had been acknowledged and corrected was the best they could come up with for firing me. However, since it was in their will, they felt that this erroneous bill was all they needed to terminate and non-renew my contract.

After the letter of termination, one board member came to me with a bribe offer to "save my job". I turned him down flat. Apparently, he did not see it like that, because he turned the telephone conversation (which he had recorded) over to the board to build their case against me. I was glad he did, because when it was played, it clearly proved that he was the one making the bribe and I was the one refusing it. You may or may not be surprised at this point to know that when I turned it over to the police as a person bribing a public official, the entire incident magically disappeared just like a bowl of magically delicious breakfast cereal.

Chapter 7
The End and the Aftermath

I will spare you all the technical details because they do not really matter. What matters is that everything the board or court asked for to verify my guilt or innocence, I willingly provided. It also matters that every single time, without fail, the proof was in my favor. You need to know that the parents and students came out in full force to support me. I know you are probably asking where they were the rest of the time. I probably would be, too, if I were you.

You need to understand that 90% of these families were black and that the majority of them were poor. The other 10% were poor white families that also could not afford private school which deemed them no better than the "blacks" in the eyes of the members of the school board and those controlling the community. These people were too busy trying to put food on the table, keep the lights and water running in their homes, making sure their kids were growing up right and safe, and working hard to keep what money they were making coming.

They did not have the time or the luxury to put themselves out there for me, no matter how much they desired to do so. But they came together at the end to say "thank you" for what I had been able to help their children accomplish, and they wanted me to know it had not gone unnoticed. For that, I will always be proud, humble, and grateful.

In the end, the appeal to the board (yes, the board that had initiated the termination against me was the same appeal body) was fruitless. It did not matter because the witnesses were too scared and intimidated to testify on my behalf. I still have correspondence from them telling me that they were sorry for letting me down but that the threats against them were too severe. Besides, they were stuck there and not able to pack up and move like I had intended to do. They would still have to live with these people and the repercussions of their actions would be lasting.

I understood then and I understand now.

I do not hold anything against any of them. Those who did testify were either demoted or left the District altogether. My feelings did not change the hell I had lived in for the past four years. This time did not suddenly disappear, though. It followed me. Twice, I was in the top two or three contenders for superintendent positions of very large urban districts. Prior to a decision being made in one district, a member of the search firm called me to report that a school board member from the District I had just left called the owner (who was also the son) of this particularly famous search firm. As a result, my name was quickly removed from the top two list that the board had selected. They told the board I had dropped out. This, of course, was not true. The second school district offered me the position, but one of the board members in Mississippi — the one who told me he would make sure that I never worked again — was obviously following my trail. He contacted the members of the school board that had just offered me the position and essentially slandered my name. The next week, this District also withdrew the offer in pure *deja vu*-style.

These incidences offered two things to me:

- that black superintendents were less likely to get a second chance and were rarely, if ever, offered a severance package; and

- that the attack on a minority's character is severe and the proverbial "black ball" is placed in the jar against them with the rest of the education world to prevent or deter them from ever working in the field again.

In fact, people in the industry I thought were my friends — even those I gave a hand up to when they needed it — would not hire or recommend me. They did not want to risk being associated with someone with a negative media-feed, even though none of the allegations in the local media were true.

Before the final blows were thrown in Mississippi, I was a sought-after speaker and presenter at conferences and seminars. Even when the accusations were being hurled left and right, I was still in demand because I was still in the seat. But once I was not there, the offers and invitations ceased. My phone calls and texts went unanswered or were completely ignored. It was shocking to see people and organizations scatter like roaches when the lights were turned on. They began to remove my name from everything and undo all of the work I had done. Once example included a program I hold near and dear to my heart. During my time there, I co-founded a nonprofit called the

Mississippi Coding Academy. I did so to build the State's technology workforce. As a result of me and several other constituents, we received $500,000 from Governor Phil Bryant and $3 million from the Kellogg Foundation. Despite my hard work in developing, designing and seeking financing for the program, in the blink of an eye, my name was removed from the website as one of the founders, as if I did not create it or that I even existed.

It was already difficult being the only black founder creating such an innovative program for the State. However, for me, it was an example that no matter how hard I worked, people loved a winner and attached themselves to a name. But, I learned that when one is down, people disassociate themselves with you and try to erase the legacy one worked so hard to establish. I will not lie, though, it was hard.

It was dang hard. But I made it. I am still standing and I am standing with my full integrity in place. As a man and as a leader, I can be proud. I knew I had to reinvent myself, though. Again… it was dang hard. It was hard to hurdle the accusations and battle slander and lies against me that were seemingly insurmountable — especially with the newspapers. Not only did they buy their ink by the barrel, but they had Google on their side. The more negative articles they printed, the higher they showed up on my digital newsfeed.

As a result, I took a little time to assess my strengths and weaknesses and decided to take a different approach to leadership because of my passion, expertise, and experience in using technology — the last of which is a field that I know focuses on talent and product.

As a result, I started a technology company so named MindAble Solutions, LLC. My first product is the award-winning *PlaBook*. The *PlaBook* is an innovative reading technology that considers how the brain works and how people are engaged in the reading process using immersive media.

As for what the future holds, only the future knows. I have continued to contribute to the field of education and leadership in numerous ways since my unfortunate experiences, but I would be lying to say it has been easy. Despite the painful difficulties and trials of those four years, I learned some valuable lessons about leadership during my time in Mississippi.

I learned:

- It is unbelievably lonely as a disruptive leader;

- A leader must deal with a lot of mental pressure and stress that comes with being the *"last line of defense"* in an organization;

- A leader must have the internal strength to deal with the judgment of the outside world about you *when*, not if, you lose;

- Leaders that aspire to live in the top 1% of life (i.e. running a business that funds your life on your own terms), the leader is going to have to work hard and give up some leisure for that to happen... depending on the ambitions;

- A leader must be fully self-aware and have the ability to navigate in life understanding these intricacies. NOTE: It is imperative to not mistake *who* you are with who you *wish* you were.

Chapter 8
Why I Would Do It All Again

"You're crazy!" is the overwhelming reply I get when I tell people that if I had it to do over again, I would. That is not to say I would not do some things differently, because I would.

Hindsight, as you know, is 20/20, and as an author-friend of mine says, "You can't go back, you can only go forward, so do not waste time looking' in the wrong direction". But all that aside, I honestly would do it again, because despite the struggles and heartaches and fear of another *Django*-style environment, the four years I spent in Mississippi were productive years and students benefitted greatly.

During my tenure as superintendent of the District:

- We won awards for our digital curriculum;

- I assisted with drafting the technology plan for the entire State of Mississippi's educational plan;

- I was asked to assist in drafting the State's curriculum evaluation system;

- Several articles were published in top tech-education publications highlighting the work that we did in the District;

- The graduation climbed from 60% to 85%;

- I co-created the first-ever Mississippi Early College dual-credit program, which puts high school students on a college campus (students in the ECDC program graduate with a high school diploma and with an associate degree from an accredited college);

- I was invited to draft the State's educators' evaluation system;

- The District had a 200% increase in student dual-enrollment (high school and college);

- The District's dropout rate was drastically reduced due to the creation of the alternative school/over-age academy for students to attend while on suspension so that they did not fall behind;

- I was nominated for Superintendent of the Year;

- Each of the four years I was there, the District worked with a balanced budget;

- The District built new facilities, including a new football field/stadium and track, that had been left in disrepair for decades;

- The District was recognized for innovation for upgrading the Wi-Fi routers to reach the school parking lot (This was the first time I was comfortable pulling up in a high school parking lot and seeing foggy windows because it was cars full of families using our internet.)

- The District put Wi-Fi in nearby parks, and even the school buses, allowing the busses to be parked in communities to light up the neighborhoods with connectivity. We wanted to give students and parents the opportunity to access the internet outside the school because a majority could not afford it on their own.

- I was the first of six national ambassadors for the U.S. Department of Education:

- I was a consultant on legislation pertaining to education in the State and assisted with drafting several education bills;

- We were the first to develop graduation pathways at the kindergarten level;

- We were the first to develop a K-12 progressive STEM curriculum;

- We won two State basketball championships.

- We were voted as one of the top 30 schools in the NATION for innovation in education using technology;

- The High School was rated a *"B"* for the first time in school history;

- The expulsion rate was at an all-time low;

- During dress-up career day, there was an overwhelming number of elementary boys of color who dressed up in suits and ties to be a "superintendent";

- The last ironic part was I was selected and went to Washington D.C. to train school board Presidents and members from all over the U.S. for the National School Board Association.

As you can see, I have plenty of reasons to be proud of my time in Mississippi, and also to be proud of the students and the change in the teachers that supported this advancement for them. I am proud of not only the accomplishments and advancements we made together, but I am also proud of the manner in which they were made.

All of this was done while facing constant criticism, slander, and danger. Yet because what was being done was both honorable and rightly motivated, we (as in the students, parents, some staff members, and support staff) were able to succeed.

I think more than anything that is what I want you to take from my story — that when you do what you do honorably and with the right motivation, you can overcome any and every obstacle put in your path. You must stay the course and never forget to keep the **main thing** the *main thing*.

Section II
Leadership Advice:
Practical Leadership

Chapter 9
Frequently Asked
Questions & Answers

What is something that's important for leaders to know from your experience?

When people can't influence you, they try to discredit you.

You put a lot of time focusing on impacting the climate of the district and the city. Why?

When I drive in Mississippi cotton grows but when I cross the state line to Tennessee, fruit trees grow. Why? Because the climate determines what grows. Therefore, the climate of your organization determines what grows in the organization. Controlling your climate is important.

It was clear that you were dramatically disruptive to the system. Why were you so purposeful about change?

To get what we want, we have to stop doing what isn't working. I believe your system is perfectly designed to get the results you are getting. A failing school is designed to fail. Every organization is designed to produce what it produces.

We have to redesign schools. If you have a pickup truck, and put lawn chairs in the back and call it a SUV, it's still not an SUV. We have schools that are designed for one thing and we are trying to use it for another. We have to redesign private companies and employers. If a kid's attendance drops from school in 8th grade because he has to stay home to watch his or her baby sister, what would you call it? What are your thoughts? You will probably call it neglect and call child family services... So, if that same 8th grade back in the days had failing attendance because they take care of their parent's farm or help with the farm, we did not call it neglect. What we did was build our education system around them so that they could work around those duties. We still use that same system today, even though it's outdated.

How did you stay focused when you were surrounded by people and a staff you could not trust?

One thing I learned long ago is that friends come and go, and that enemies accumulate. Success matters. You have to stay focused on what makes a difference. You have to figure out what issues you are willing to die for. Be cognizant of the fact that not everything is.

Why did so many teachers complain?

Low morale is a result of changing performance expectations. The board demands the schools to go from low to high, then the superintendent sets expectations for the principal, then the principal sets the expectations for teachers, and if allowed, TEACHERS complain to the BOARD. But the point is, on any job when you raise the bar, the morale tends to go south.

How did you get so many people to buy into the vision, as well as get the board to approve so many different items?

The easiest way to explain is that you sell the problem, not the solution.

There was a struggle between you and this board because you wanted to move at a faster pace than they did. Why?

As I told my board, I am willing to take longer than expected, but students do not have the luxury of time. How long do you want to wait if a student is getting a poor education?

Although you were hands-on, you still allowed other people to make decisions. How did that work?

An administrator's job is to see that decisions are made. I believe in empowering the chain of command. I believe that the lowest paid person in the chain with the power to make decisions should be the one to make it. For example, let the janitor decide on what wax to use on the floors. That should not have to come from the administration. I ensured decisions were being made, and that people who understood them were making them under oversight, rather than by people far up in the chain of command.

Your staff did not like your speech about being a team — not a family. They did not like that. Why not?

Yes, I rhetorically asked if their school was a family. Then, I reminded them that the first order of business of a family is to take care of the weak and to protect one another. I did not want that. Our students did not need that — rather, could not afford that. I said I wanted to be a TEAM, because the first order of business of a team is to win. Everyone plays their part to the best of their ability and even so we only advance only those that perform the best. I also reminded them that on a team, you either grow or *go*.

In the beginning, you used data to display the district's failures. Why take that approach?

I did so because, *"Success has many fathers, but failure is an orphan..."*. Failure is not a bad thing, when but I tried to get them to their failures in order for change to happen, it did not go well. Accepting accountability for the good and the bad causes change, so you need to always be open to critique.

You did a lot of staff recognition and celebrations. Why?

I believe you need to recognize and celebrate the small successes. It's an incremental approach to receive exponential results. We needed to build this brick by brick. I believed we needed to do 1% better each day than we did the day before.

There was a lot of changes to be made. How did you accomplish it without frustrating people and causing them to feel all the change at once?

My job was to break the job down into smaller pieces so that it could be done right. If you dive in a pool and belly flop, it is painful. But if you dive in hands first, pain isn't an issue. The reason for that is because you gave the water time to adjust. You 'invaded' it a little at a time. You cannot force too much change on people all at once. Remember, you can only go as fast as the vision is influenced and funded.

The bar was raised which resulted in a lot of leaders resigning. What happened?

One of the key problems with urban education is that motivation itself is one of the largest determiners for success, and character is difficult to teach. Urban leaders become exposed when expectations are set and therefore they are held accountable to those expectations. Urban leadership is not a place to coast. I believe you raise the standards and do not water it down for diversity. There is not one certain way you educate *"black,"* kids but socioeconomics and poverty levels matter.

What do you suggest is the roadmap to successful innovation implementation?

There is absolutely no roadmap. The world is changing, and the paths others have followed will not prepare you for the leadership tasks of the future. It is even suggested that tomorrow's leader should not emulate today's. I am often asked, *"How do you lead in innovation when there is no path?"* I believe you shoot first and aim later. Too often in education, we are discussing the same issues that were being discussed 5 to 10 years ago. We need to be more about action.

Why do you not believe the principal is the instructional leader? Isn't the building leader the highest expert of instruction?

The Principal is not the instructional leader; they are the leaders of instructors. One person cannot be the expert of the collective group. Then, there would be too many different subject matter experts. It's becomes the Principal vs Professional Learning Communities. The principal should invest in PLCs. The PLCs ramps up instruction better than any single person. The Principal's job is to improve the group of teachers and not to micromanage one teacher. I do believe the Principal needs to be the Lead Learner. They are to set the example by way of continuous improvement.

Not being afraid to have critical conversations and coaching people up was a hallmark of your leadership. Why?

I feel that what we do not address, we endorse. Your culture is nothing more than what you teach and tolerate as a leader. The greatest injustice you can do is to allow unproductive folks feel comfortable in your system.

How did you deal with all the negative people?

I believe that you have to speak to your *"Whispering Shadows."* Self-talk is one of the top tools a leader should have to navigate a healthy mind in the mist of their leadership. Whispering shadows are the negative talk you play in your mind repeatedly. They can destroy you as a person if you do not learn how to talk back to them.

The leadership beliefs that embodied your administration always had a technology undertone as you looked to disrupt education on a local and national level.

Yes, because we should be educating children for their future and not our past. School does a great job of preparing kids for a world that no longer exist. Computers have simply evolved faster than our education system over the past few decades, and our race for getting an education is falling behind. If everything is changing that fast, then there is no standardized path — you have to prepare kids for the path and not one path. You have to personalize learning. When there is a monumental moment, a person gets out of their phone and takes a picture or video, but this does not happen in our classrooms. The practices outside the institutions are happening faster than inside the institutions or schools. As of now, we are not in the dark, but we are in a dimly lit room. We have to move forward because one day, the world will be changing so fast, we will no longer be able to learn from our past. There will be principals, but that's it. This is close to where we are now. We are at a point when the rate of change outside of an organization is greater than the rate of change inside of an organization, and that signifies the end is near.

You put an emphasis on shifting the culture using technology. But from a global perspective, technology hasn't impacted education cultural. Why?

Education has developed a different culture. In education, we have not developed a culture of growth-inspired change as much as we have fostered a culture of accountability. Technology breeds creativity-inspired updates, and education seems to be forcing compliance-based updates that do not lead to better outcomes. Even with the influx of devices streaming into our schools, we still have a culture of compliance, so technology hasn't made the impact on education as it should.

We still have too many teachers that are talking too much while students sit in the classroom talking too little. Even more so at urban schools, we are stuck between innovation and the poverty of teaching basic skills. It's the urban education's pitfall. People are asking if innovation can happen at our nation's urban schools. I demonstrated that innovation can and needs to happen for the success of our nation and world.

When you build your team, what type of person do you look for?

Over the years, I have heard a lot of people talk about the importance of hiring problem-solvers. I try to hire problem-avoiders. If you do not create problems, you do not have to solve them. You also have to be strategic. If you find yourself making every decision based on your gut, you had better be on a battlefield. Data analysis is too pervasive and accessible for you to rely on your base instincts.

You change the school curriculum to include the Four C's: Critical thinking, collaboration, communication and creativity. You have to make them globally relevant. What was the significance?

As educators, we should develop human intelligence and not just train people to work in industrial jobs.

Any general words of wisdom on what makes for successful leadership?

Over the years, I have heard a lot of people talk about the importance of hiring problem-solvers. I try to hire problem-avoiders. If you do not create problems, you do not have to solve them. You must also be, in some sense, strategic. You need to occasionally stop and think about what needs to be done to bring about long-term sustainable changes that propel you in the right direction. As I just said, if you find yourself making every decision based on your gut, you had better be on a battlefield.

Why do you think leadership is hard for some people?

Because people are not following their gift. I believe you should follow you gift, not your passion. Be confident in the gift God gave you.

Your leadership was impacted by a lot of setbacks before you succeed.

As Dr. Martin Luther King stated, *"The line towards progress is never straight."*

You decided to do an overhaul of policies upon arrival. Why was that a good leadership decision?

The time to make rules is when you do not need them.

A lot of energy was put into nontraditional professional development that was more than a sit and get.

Yes, the regimen of Navy SEAL teams inspires building the capacity of your staff. They must constantly train in the field. It must be job-embedded and constant.

The Central Office you inherited was a top-down administration, and you changed their philosophy. Why?

I believe the leadership of the central office is meant to be a service center. Leadership is not about being the best, but about making people better around you. Top down leadership has a price. You must lead horizontally. You must get as much power as you can get from leading at the top. As a great leader, you must understand that you are not the one walking the halls, cleaning the buildings, cooking the food and teaching the kids. You have to have a presence at every level to be a great leader so that the people who actually *do* these things do not feel neglected.

You were a very involved leader

Yes, I believe you should watch what a person does, not what they say. There are sometimes contradictions with what people say vs. their action and what the data tells us. So, I had to observe what was going on in the buildings more and spend less time in meetings.

In your role as a leader you seemed to align everyone on the same page. What did you say or do to accomplish this?

A leader's best friend is *"clarity."* People need to know where you stand.

As a leader, you were persistence about putting all the data in context instead of just presenting all the data.

Something like $500 is data, but you must consider the context and value of it. For example, if my daughter's weekly allowance was $500 you would say that's a lot. If I say $500 is my total net worth, you would say that's bad. Data is nothing without understanding the context.

I do believe as a leader you do not just sit back and let a person fail the organization.

If a bus is going to crash and you have the option to stop it by grabbing the steering wheel, you grab the steering wheel.

We should never make excuses or accept partial or mediocre performance.

For example, we say, *"She's a good teacher but..."* A good teacher is a good instructor, good with parents, volunteers for after school events that do not necessarily involve her students, is good with the students in the hallways, with colleagues, and is, well, just all-around good.

You were very strict on evaluations, hiring the right candidate and coaching the wrong candidates out. Why?

Even when a district is experiencing a teacher shortage — quantity or quality wise — you should never hire the best of a bad lot. In fact, when we lost teachers and the board complained no one wanted to work for me, I would tell the board we were losing the best mediocre teachers in the business. I strived to raise expectations because I believe students always deserve the best.

You appeared to be a calculated leader?

Yes, I believe you need to be strategic about change. You do not ever tear down a fence until you know why it was built.

What did you instill in your leaders?

I tried to instill the fact that as educators, we are leaders with the ability to inspire people. Knowledge alone isn't enough these days. You must inspire people. I assumed then, and still do, that everybody wants to be the best they can be. But the human instinct in some people is to do little more than survive. They just want to be average. As educators, we need to inspire them to want more than that — to know they deserve and are capable of more than that.

That's why people like Eric Thomas, Gary V., and other leaders like them are so impactful to company organization.

Urban leadership is difficult. What type of leader do you look for?

You have to be able to paint pictures. If they do not see it, they can't follow it. Great leaders know it's is going to be a long, hard grind. I believe every leader needs to have an un-relenting belief that kids can be successful, no matter what their background is. We need to realize that if we assume poor kids can't be successful, a lot of people in your district or organization would not be there. You might even be one of them.

We have to understand that equity is not about making sure that every kid is getting the same thing, but it's making sure every kid is getting what they need. The leader in an urban environment must realize that it's not enough to get people on the right bus and in the right seat. It's usually a fast train ride on which we are all on the same train, on the same track, going in the same direction. We are just in different cars of the train.

Why did you invent the K16 Instructional Technology Integration (ITI) model?

Most people lead with devices. I believe with technology, you must lead with an instructional model in place.

Would some people say you do not support the adults and that you are student centered?

I believe we should support and serve our staff. With that said, I do believe the job of the school is to make things easy for the students instead of the adults.

The one thing you screamed the loudest was "educating the whole child." Why should schools do this?

Focusing on teacher preparation and a stronger curriculum is not going to get us anywhere unless we pay attention to the most basic needs of these children — things like nutrition, health and safety, and the instability of the homes. These needs must be met for optimal learning to take place.

Most people downplay the effects of poverty. What would you say to them?

I would ask if they had ever lived in a housing project, or an area of high crime? Were they poor? Did they have asthma? In other words, I would try to get them to empathize and identify with the situation. I did not miss school much either — partly because my answers to these questions is *"no."* We lived in a community that made it easy to be a good student.

What are your beliefs on the disparities of some districts?

I consider the difference to be like broken sticks and rocks vs. manicured lawns. Differences are the environmental influences on schools. When we talk about the future for our own children, we think and talk in terms of years. But when it comes to children in poverty, we think and talk in terms of the next day. Their environment shapes their thinking.

For a child growing up in the hood, using sticks to hit rocks and other such activities is counterintuitive to success in our current classrooms. The haphazard chaos in real life carries over into a lack of organizational skills, discipline, no respect for authority, no emotional regulation, and a lack of focus on anything but their own immediate needs. Growing up with a manicured lawn is different. Everything is orderly and in its place. You know what to expect and you know what is expected of you. Ultimately, one's environment and experiences can drastically shape what a person believes is possible in their world.

What happens when a system is so poor that it's full of rocks and sticks kids. Well, it is unable to look any farther than the next day. Just get through the day... that's all it focuses on. This can't continue. We need to make sure every district gives their kids an *"Etch-a-Sketch"* education by shaking up the old model so that we can forget about it and give every student a future.

You built a lot of celebration, hype, and excitement around children

Yes, I did. Children are our product. The education system is the only entity that does not get excited about its product. This is the only corporate giant that does not get excited about the product that it's producing.

We should care about the learner experience like the video game industry cares about user experience. I believe we should be excited and proud of something like a child reading or graduating, just like Sony is about their video games or Jay Z is about his album.

You focused a lot on urgency. You put a lot of energy on time and the use of it. Why?

Life is all about time and once it's spent, you can't get it back. We do not think time is important until it is about to run out. Education is about time and right now, there is a lot of it being wasted that we can't get back. Kids are literarily sitting in classrooms day after day and learning nothing. We are also not being as flexible with our time as we should be. Every child given the right instruction can master the content given enough time. We need to structure education to work with that. Our graduation rates are our end goal, but we need to spend every day of our school time investing in our graduates.

Communication is important because it allows you to get feedback from constitutes

One thing I learned early-on is that the more you know about your students, the better you are as a teacher. I learned that if my students are successful, I am going to be successful. The same thing applies to a principal. If your faculty's successful, you're going to be successful, and if my principals are successful, I am going to be successful.

But really, it all comes back to the students or customers. The more the students are engaged in the work, the better results you're going to get. This means you've got to make things as relevant for them as soon as possible and for that to work, there must be a feedback loop. The same goes for upper level leaders.

You really pushed for everyone having the belief that all children can succeed. Please explain?

I truly believe that you have to see past a child's present state. The first question I would challenge yourself to ask about your student is, *"Who do you see?"*

The second would be what your aspirations are for that student, and do they change based on their dress, how they look, or who their parents are? These questions are important because we are the last chance for kids. If we give up, who do they have left? So, do not put a kid out of your class and say I do not want you back. Send them out and tell them I am going to send you out, but we will need to figure this out because I want you to be successful in this class. It is important that we get this right because our kids represent 20% of our population, but 100% of our future.

You led a student-centered organization and you wanted students involved in every aspect of their leaving.

Yes — the students are our customers and education is the one industry that does not communicate with its customer... it does not provide an end-point to students or their parents.

What are your thoughts on technology replacing jobs and, in your case, teachers?

I believe history has told us a lot about disruptive forces. The record was disrupted by the tape. The CDs disrupted the tape, and the CDs in turn were disrupted by the iPod. Education is also facing disruptive forces, which is technology. Those things that can adapt will survive. I told my staff technology will not replace teachers, but those who use it will replace those who do not. Our students are prepped more for tangible results and less for a lifetime of learning. I have learned that you can't save time, store time, nor stretch time. We have to keep in mind that our present time is short, but the future is forever. This means that children's present time is a short 13 years (K-12), but their future adult life is long.

That's why I believe we need to take a first-year teacher and make them more like a fifth-year year teacher as quickly as possible, because students can't afford to wait.

We always say that we are preparing kids for the future, but I firmly believe the future was yesterday and we are already late. That's why I focused on what we are doing the very millisecond a child walks through our doors to the very minute they leave. We need be purposeful and take advantage of the entire time they are in our care.

You were relentless on holding principles accountable. Why?

Because no organization can rise above their leadership. In a successful organization, a leader takes people where they would not normally go. The reason is because people first buy into the leader and then they buy into the vision. The catch is people won't go along with you if they can't get along with you. You have to connect with them, and good leaders are connectors. Therefore, the most important person in a school district is the principal based on recent research. If you have good teachers and a bad principal, then the staff's performance gets worst. Conversely, if you have weak teachers and a great principal, the staff ability improves. This is why we can't afford to have weak principals. The best example of this leadership in action is the LeBron James Effect. LeBron can change the completive level of any basketball team. He has consistently shown that he can take a non-contender team and make them the top in their division.

Only in school systems is leadership about validation, but in the real world, leadership is about standing on your own and making unpopular decisions. I even believe the principal should have to prove why they keep their teachers, janitors, secretary, etc. If that person does not add to the district or add to children, then we do not need them.

You always educated your board and you made recommendations to them instead of just telling them what to do. Why?

School boards are different than most. The board lives in the community, and truthfully the students and monies they are overseeing are theirs to begin with. Therefore, do not protect your board from their decisions. If you do, they will attach a bad decision to you.

Also, you need to memo upwards. If the board gives you oral instructions to do something and it's not put in writing, then after you do it, send a memo back to all the board members stating, based on a directive from "_____" Board member, as a status report. Be specific and always report at the board meeting. You just have to realize that when you want to go one direction, and you have a board that wants to go in a different direction, you have to go in their direction.

You moved a lot of leaders out of failing schools and specifically chose leaders from successful buildings to replace those leaders. Why?

I believe it takes a lot to turn around a failing school or business. I have always said we have to make an extraordinary effort, and ordinary people can't do this.

Do you believe you were overly optimistic in taking on a district and community in such bad shape?

No, I feel that most leaders live in a small box. They think they can't influence or change things a lot. I call that a limited leadership life. I have never accepted that. I believe every leader should reject that philosophy so that they can actually change things. If you embrace a philosophy that says you are limitless when it comes to making change, you can put your ding in the universe.

That's why I felt I was able to take on the challenge in Mississippi. This is a huge arc of my life. It's what drives me to have big ideas that lead to actions. We must embed this non-acceptance of the status quo into our leadership life.

Also, I would encourage people to remember these things as well:

- No matter how gifted you are as a leader, you can't move systems by yourself. You can't do great things alone;

- You need to share leadership; meaning people who are serving with you are partners — not subjects;

- Your leadership will be exposed. What you do will be talked about — for better or worse;

- You must have horizontal leadership. Be warned, we stand on the platform all day, but we are not higher than our people;

- We must be able to inspire people to believe that it's a mutual vision to work towards a goal;

- Leadership matters. How leaders lead matters. A leader's heart matters. Leadership is not all hands-off, but it's not always about having your hand in everything, either. It requires an ability to handle delicate balance;

- The best thing a leader can do is empower people.

Section III
Research: Theoretical
Leadership

Chapter 10
Data/Assessment/ Accountability (Quality Assurance, School Improvement)

This module focuses on the administrator's ability to use various forms of data to inform practice, decisions, and efforts toward overall improvement. Assessment is a word used commonly in the field of education. The administrator must possess the ability to create a quality assurance system that effectively assesses each component of his/her role as an administrator. This quality assurance system should include ways to assess the quality of teacher instruction, student learning, the academic climate of the school, and meeting established targets and goals.

The administrator must engage in the ongoing and continuous improvement of the school. Even if your school is one of the top schools, there is always room for improvement. The improvement should involve a close look at the school-wide data and information.

Topics within this Chapter:

- Establishing/Understanding the Mission and Vision of your school that includes all stakeholders;
- Establish a school-wide vision for the quality assurance (assessment) system;
- Creating a quality assurance system (formative and summative assessments);
- Collecting and analyzing data for improvement.
- Sharing data with stakeholders; and
- Creating a plan for improvement.

Educational institutions at all levels are one of the most important places that shape the future of the country by educating the next generation. This is why it is really important that our educational systems be thoroughly monitored, and improvements should be implemented wherever they are necessary.

In fact, there is a dire need for this to happen. It does not matter if the institution you are working in is one of the best in the state; there is always room for improvement. Therefore, every level of an educational institution should have an assessment system that compiles all the necessary data regarding each department and then evaluate the overall performance. The person that should be responsible to establish such a system is the administrator. The administrator is one of the most important people that oversees the overall day-to-day operations of his or her institution. Everything related goes through the administrator, which means they have the most knowledge regarding how the system of the institution works. This is why the most qualified person to establish an assessment system for all the staff hired is the administrator.

The reason why the administrator is the most qualified person for this job is because they have the ability to collect all the necessary data required to develop a particular assessment system. This is where the leadership part of an administrator at any education institutional level begins. The administrator for each department should establish certain targets and goals. The departments should then work towards achieving these targets and goals throughout the academic year. This will not only improve the quality of the education system of the school but may also benefit the school system financially.

Other than students and the school staff, the administrator should also be responsible to keep the stakeholders happy with the overall performance of the school. The best way to ensure that the school is running in the right direction is by developing a system that actually monitors the overall performance of the entire school. The people who have invested in the school expect it to deliver, and a good assessment system will surely keep them satisfied as they will be able to view the performance themselves.

A school's quality of education is directly reflected by its students. Therefore, assessment of the teachers and the students' performance should be one of the top priorities while developing this system. There should be a way to assess the quality of the teacher's instructions to the students. There should also be a system to assess the students' performance other than the regular examination system.

Developing such a system should not be a difficult task in today's age. We are living in a modern age of technology and have definitely escaped the world of paper registers. Every important data in almost every industry today is stored in the digital form. Therefore, the administrator should also work on developing the system in a digital form. In this way, it will be a lot easier to manage and assess the entire school system.

Establishing/Understanding the Mission and Vision of Your School That Includes all Stakeholders

Before the administrator starts working on the development of this assessment system, they need to understand the main mission of the school that they are working for. They should make sure that the entire school system is moving in the same direction. One way to make sure is by developing a system that directs them toward their mission and also assesses their performances along the way.

Imagine you want to plan a trip to the beach with a couple of your friends. All three of you will coordinate through phone call, texting or emails and then plan everything to do in the trip. The trip will most likely go smoothly and you will have a lot of fun together. The reason for that is because all three of you had developed a mission beforehand and then accomplished it by going on a trip. Similarly, to run a big organization such as a school, it needs to have a mission that all departments should be obliged to follow.

Every school has proper mission and vision that they need to follow to achieve their targets. The administrator should be able to understand each and every mission of each department and then make sure that everyone stays on course.

The administrator should also be able to establish the mission and vision of the school if they are not properly defined. The first thing you need to understand is that mission and vision are two different things. The vision is the ultimate goal that everyone strives to achieve, while the mission is simply the direction and path required to achieve that particular goal.

To establish a vision for your school you have to do the following things:

- **Establishing a Vision:** Without a proper vision, the school will clearly lack the direction. The administrator must bring the superintendent/principal and the stakeholders on board when drafting the vision statement. The whole group should decide the ultimate goal that the school wants to achieve in a certain amount of time. It could be the improvement of teaching quality or an infrastructure development to provide facilities. Whatever the vision is, it must be drafted for the future with a time limit to achieve it.

- **Eliminate Obstacles:** If the vision of the school displays a drastic change, then there will be some obstacles in the way that need to be removed. One of the biggest obstacles is the fear of change that automatically occurs when people are told to step out of their comfort zone. You need to ensure all the staff and shareholders that it will be easy to adapt to the vision once the time arrives.

- **Share Examples of Vision:** It is highly likely that the change you are proposing in the vision is taken from a successful competitor or it is simply just "trending" so that you have to move with the time. However, the best way to convince the school staff and the stakeholders is by showing them the examples of the similar changes that have brought success in other organizations. For example, if your vision is to build a new and bigger library, then you need to show the evidence of the other schools that have improved the academic standard by building a new library.

To accomplish the vision that you are setting, you need a mission for the entire school to follow. Below are some of the ways you can do it:

- **Establishing the Mission Statement:** After you have laid out the vision for the school, by getting it approved by the management and stakeholders, you need to draft a mission statement in order to achieve the said the vision. Mission statements are simply the actions that the entire school needs to take in order to reach the vision, which is laid out for the betterment of the institution.

- **Getting everyone on the Board to Follow the Mission:** Presenting the mission is one thing but getting people to follow it is an entirely different ball game. The administrator needs to ensure that all the staff and the students are on the same page before imposing the mission on them. Every person associated with the institute needs to understand that in order to get to their vision, they will be required to follow a certain mission. For example, let's say your school's vision is to improve culture and social needs for students with a diverse background. The mission to accomplish this goal will be required to make some drastic changes to the school's curriculum. It might also be required to introduce categories such as social events that educate the students on diversity and different cultures.

Establish a School-Wide Vision for the Quality Assurance (Assessment) System

After getting the approval from the management and stakeholders for the vision, you need to officially establish it for everyone associated with the school. Teachers and students should also be informed regarding the school's decision to aim for the vision that is to have a perfectly working quality assurance system.

All the departments of the school should be assigned various tasks so that they can contribute to achieving the vision, which is a perfect quality assurance system. The system should be developed to assess all the necessary data that can help you understand and then improve any aspect of the school. You need to figure out whether you need to hire some new staff particularly for this system or you just need a software that will take care of everything. Consult the experts who have helped implement these systems before in other school or organization.

Creating a Quality Assurance System (Formative and Summative Assessments)

As we mentioned earlier, the quality of every school is reflected through its students. Therefore, it is really important to focus on the student learning outcomes as the main goal that needs to be improved the most.

Many schools already have quality assurance systems that are traditional and have remained unchanged for decades. If you are the administrator, then you need to look for changes in these systems in order to improve the students' learning outcomes.

There are two major types of quality assurance systems that can be commonly found in the schools:

- Formative Assessments Systems
- Summative Assessment Systems

Formative Assessment System

Formative assessment systems are designed to directly monitor the students' learning process. This assessment is done by getting feedback from the students so that the instructors can improve their teaching tactics accordingly. These assessments usually have low stakes, which means they are just formalities and there is no competition among the students, unlike the tests and examinations.

Formative assessments have several benefits, such as:

- It helps students identify their strengths and weaknesses.

- It helps them target a specific area, which needs improvements.

- It helps the instructors recognize the struggles of their students so that they can address their problems and work on improving them.

Here are some examples of formative assessments:

- After each lecture, ask the students to draw a concept map regarding their understanding of the topic.

- Ask the students to list the main points from the lecture that they just received.

- Ask them to submit a research proposal for early feedback.

Summative Assessment System

The summative assessment system is definitely the most common assessment program and can be found in almost every school in the world. This assessment is done by the end of a benchmark or an academic season. These assessments have a high stake, which means that they are of great value and create competition among students as well to perform the best.

Here are some of the examples of the summative assessment system:

- Class quizzes

- Midterm Examinations

- Final Examinations

- Final Project

- Research Paper

There is a still a lot of room for improvement in both formative and summative systems. You have to figure out a way to get the best out of the students without putting too much pressure on them.

Collecting and Analyzing Data for Improvement

Working toward a vision requires thorough research and in-depth analysis of the current state of the school. Therefore, you need to collect as much data as possible so that it can be improved accordingly.

The administrator needs to develop a feedback system that can deliver performance figures of all the staff of the school including the instructors and students. The quality assurance systems, such as the formative and summative assessments systems, which were mentioned earlier, should also be able to collect some useful data that can be utilized to analyze the overall students' performance.

After analyzing the data on students' performance, the teachers should also be asked to deliver some feedback regarding the performance of their students. They should inform the administrator of each and every detail about the students and also give their suggestions on whether the weaknesses of the students can be improved. After receiving the necessary data from all the departments of the school, the administrator should analyze it in-depth and identify the ways to improve each and every sector that directly or indirectly affects the performance of the students. All the compiled data should definitely help find the shortcomings and weaknesses in the current system of the school. These weaknesses can then be avoided when developing a new quality assurance system.

Sharing the Data with Stakeholders

The most important people that have the final say for the big change in the system that the administrator is working on are definitely the shareholders. The shareholders decide whether or not you should move forward with the development of the new system for the school. Therefore, you need to convince them with evidence that should be in the form of data, which reflects the weaknesses in the current system.

After collecting the data and analyzing it in-depth, the entire information should be converted into a report and then presented to the shareholders. The report should be convincing enough and should highlight the room for improvement in each department that affects the students' overall performance. The shareholders' approval is probably the most important thing that you need to get in order to proceed towards your vision. They are basically part-owners of the school and any big change simply cannot happen under their noses. Therefore, the report prepared by the administrator should have valid reasons and be convincing enough to grab the shareholders' attention and also get their approval stamp.

Creating a Plan for Improvement

After getting the nod from the shareholders and the upper management of the school, the administrator should immediately begin working on creating the improvement plan. Since the vision would be set by this stage, you just have to create a proper plan and follow the mission to reach the ultimate improvement goal.

For example, if the school's ultimate goal for improvement is to build a robotics laboratory where young children can learn to code and build robots, then you should definitely plan ahead for this project. You should hire an architect, an engineer and also most importantly, find a place in or around the school where the lab can be built.

After the construction, you need to get the right furniture and equipment so that the kids can fully utilize the newly built lab that is particularly built to expand their learning skills.

Schools are changing with time as we advance toward the new generation that is exposed to modern technology right after they are born. Teaching these kids with the same old curriculum and style that we went through will never be enough, therefore every school should always be looking for improvements that can be made and then act upon it accordingly.

Chapter 11
Technology Leader

Incorporating technology properly into any organization or any institution is important when carrying out daily functions. Different activities like management of data, personnel duties, research activities, meetings, communication, and finances all depend upon the people handling technology in the relevant fields.

This is specifically true for educational institutions where the technology is not only being used by students, faculty, staff, and administrators on a daily basis for on-time delivery of instructions and learning of content. In many situations, technology can also be used by educators to teach various subjects to students as their course requirements.

Due to this focus on technology as a tool for instruction, leadership and direction become important for this area. Technology leader in this situation can help the institution or the organization manage, plan, implement, and evaluate the technology's effectiveness when serving many purposes.

Technology leader plays an important role in establishing a foundation in an institution that assists individuals and encourages them to use technology effectively in order to sustain its use. Effective use of technology and leadership work together go hand in hand. If technology and leadership are handled as separate entities, the tasks to achieve the goals of an institution or an organization will definitely fail.

In a world full of big data and analytics, trusting only on your gut to make important decisions is not enough. Most organizations feel that data should be the basic reason of an organization's decision-making. According to PwC's Global Data and Analytics Survey, using data more often and effectively remains more theoretical rather than practical.

Advancements in modern technology like CD-ROMs, videotapes, flash drives, networks, printers, scanners and computers, and the growing internet technology have affected schools and its education system in many ways. They have increased the access to education, reduced the cost of instruction, helped develop learner-centered education and improved the quality of education through interactive learning.

The most obvious and important technological impact on schools is the global access to education. The internet has virtually removed the geographical and time isolation across the globe. Students around the world now have access to education on their own convenience, therefore eliminating the traditional brick-and-mortar education model. One more example of technology connecting people is that of Webinars. Schools and educational institutes can conduct international meeting through a Webinar.

Although the technology of video chatting with people has existed for quite some time, however Webinars are somewhat different since they give official guests or motivational speakers a platform to connect directly to the audience. GoToWebinar and BrightTALK are two examples where technology has made it easier for organizations to connect with each other. In the same way, there are even more technologies that allow organizations to connect with other organizations in the same field.

Despite these technological breakthroughs, the path to accepting newer technologies in schools has been quite slow. Schools and educational institutes have been finding it hard to implement new technologies right away. Therefore, schools are hesitant to adopt newer ways as they think that these machines are complicated tools. Although the majority of the administrators want to become data-driven, only 61% say that their institutes are somewhat data-driven in their decision-making. With technology overtaking almost every aspect of a business or an institute, it is thoughtful to use the data it generates to see what is happening in your institute and use the information to make the institute more active by testing out different kinds of scenarios and their success.

Let us look at the five ways to be more data-driven.

Strategy

Data-driven decision-making starts with the all-important strategy. This helps focus all your attention by filtering out data that is not helpful for your school. The first step is to identify your goals. This indicates that you are looking for new ways to implement a more effective educational system or you want to know what works and what does not.

Take a look at your school or District's objectives and develop a strategy around them. By doing so you will not be surprised by the possibilities that big data has in hand for you.

Identify Key Areas

Data flows into an organization or institution from all directions. This includes from student-teacher interactions to the machines being used by your staff. It is necessary that you manage multiple sources of data and recognize which areas will be the most beneficial. Identify which area is the key to achieve an overarching business strategy. This could be for any purpose, for example, finance or operations department of an institution.

Data Targeting

Now that you have identified which areas of your school will benefit the most from analytics and the issues that you want to focus on, it is time that you target which data sets will answer those questions.

This includes looking at the data that you have and finding which data provides you with the most valuable information. Keep in mind that when different departments use different systems, it can lead to inaccurate data reporting. The best systems can cross-analyze data from different sources.

Collecting and Analyzing Data

Identify the key staff members who will be managing the data first-hand. These members are mostly the heads of different departments. The most useful data will be collected at all levels and should come from both internal and external sources. This is so that you can have an all-around view of what is going on across the organization.

To analyze the data effectively, you will need integrated systems that will connect you to all the different data sources. The level of skills you will need will differ as per what you need to analyze. The more difficult the problem, the more specialists you will need.

Sometimes simple analytics may need no more than a little knowledge of Excel, but some analytic platforms offer easy accessibility so that everyone can easily access data to help connect the entire workforce.

Turning Insights into Action

The way you present the insights that you have gained from the data will determine how much you can earn from them. There are a number of intelligence tools that can be implemented in a school system in ways that will make your insights more digestible for important decisions to be made.

Establishing a School-Wide Vision of Technology

In the 21st century, children seem to be born with an electronic device in their hand. But is it a good idea to have children dealing with electronic devices at such an early age? Most experts agree that children under the age of three do not need to be exposed to electronic devices. But then again, research shows that there are positive effects of technology on the child's learning and development in a cognitive and social manner.

When a child turns three, they progress into a new stage of development. First, it includes concrete learners to stay interested in speaking, writing, drawing, and numbers. Children at this age are active and mobile, and they require frequent changes and physical experiences. Technology being used in the classroom can meet the needs of these development changes like exploration, changing play styles, and working at their own pace.

Students have the tendency to learn in different ways. Technology can help the students in differentiating by giving all the students the opportunity to succeed by allowing them to work on projects at their own pace. Technology can also help disabled students and enrich the advanced students.

The use of the internet introduces education to a whole new world of educational resources. Movies, films, video clips, etc. are now available only at a single click. These resources can be used to enhance the learning and teaching standards and provide the students with an alternative teaching strategy to enrich the development of advanced students in the classroom.

Technology today has become an important part of how we work and live. Teaching students how to use technology in terms of learning, research, collaboration and problem-solving will help them prepare for the careers they choose ahead. It can help reduce the fear of new technologies being introduced in the future and familiarizing them with each tool. The more familiar students are, the easier it is for them to use computers and its systems as they enter to their diverse fields.

Here are 5 reasons why technology should be incorporated into the classrooms:

Engages Students and Creates Active Learners

By using an electronic device, whether a computer, tablet or any other device, it encourages self-directed learning and creates active participants in the learning process instead of just passive learners that are found in a lecture environment. Interactive lesson plans help turn boring subjects into fun and engaging subjects for students.

Encourages Individual Learning and Growth

No one learns at the same pace; however, technology can help set the pace at an individual level in the classroom. For example, technology can provide accommodations for struggling and disabled students such as virtual lesson plans. Students can learn on their own pace, review concepts on their own or even skip as needed. Access to the internet also gives students wide access to a broad range of resources to conduct research.

Facilitates Peer Collaboration

In a research that has been conducted by the U.S. Department of Education, many educators had reported that technology had facilitated peer collaboration. They had noted that when students were assigned to small groups for technology-based projects, students that already had the right equipment assisted less-skilled students. Peer tutoring, mentoring and collaboration were one of the unexpected results of technology.

Prepare Students for the Real World

Technology is an important part of our everyday lives. Teaching students how to use technology for learning, research, collaboration, and problem-solving will prepare them for their future careers.

Creates More Engaged and Successful Teachers

Using different technologies like virtual lesson plans can help free some time both when developing and delivering the curriculum. This allows the teachers to spend more time with those students who are struggling, ensuring that the entire class is prepared for tests and exams.

The Role of the Principal in Being the Technology Leaders

Being a principal of a 21st-century school, you will need a good amount of leadership in technology. Being a leader of technology requires the willingness to learn, flexibility and the capacity to accept change on a regular basis.

Adaptability and acceptance of ambiguity are necessary. Technology changes at a fast pace and there is no list of things that must be done and things that are a must to have. Leaders of technology need to be lifelong learners and explorers of new, exciting, and useful technology.

With constant changes taking place in the education sector, the role of the leaders is also changing at a fast pace. Leadership is the key component when it comes to guiding the teaching-learning process and for preparing today's students with the relevant knowledge and skills. The leaders play an important role in technology integration. This role is crucial in helping teachers create today's ideal learning environment for students.

The principal's diverse roles have always been a part of a long tradition of expectations and responsibilities. The recent addition to the roles of a principal is being a technology leader. The special challenge for the principal is to be a technology leader and to encourage the development of teachers and students. Principals who are comfortable with technology become models that teachers follow. Principals demonstrate their use of technology with e-mail, websites, preparing reports with graphs and pictures, preparing presentations, using the student information system to track everyday operations of the school, and using handheld devices to complete teacher appraisals. Principals who are technology leaders showcase the uses of technology during meetings. They invite teacher demonstrations of technology integration in lessons or in staff meetings. The displays of student and classroom use of technology are prominent in their schools. Leaders of technology encourage the implementation of technology in instructional strategies. Principals note the teachers' use of technology integration in their lessons.

They help teachers establish goals for implementation of technology in instructional strategies. The principal is responsible to defuse the fear and the resistance while using technology. One of the best methods of inspiring the use of technology is by influencing other teachers. Principal's visibility and support for teachers are essential. Monitoring the attainment of school goals is the principals' responsibility. Therefore, they need to work to remove roadblocks for the use of technology in order to assure that teachers do not lose interest or become frustrated by the expectations of technology.

Below are some of the crucial roles and responsibilities of a school leader for the effective integration of technology:

Establish the Vision and Goals

The leader must play the role of a *"visionary"* to build the context for technology in the school and understand how technology can be used to rearrange the learning environment. In doing so, leaders will help in empowering teachers and help students use technology wisely.

Model Use of Technology

If you start using it, they will start using it as well. The leaders always take the lead and make the team follow. Use technology in your workspace and set an example of effectively using technology and how efficient things get.

Support Technology Use in the School

Leaders need to take initials and attend different training sessions about the use and applications of new technologies. Leaders need to practice the use of these resources so that they can discuss it with their staff. Look for training opportunities for teachers through attendance at these sessions.

Professional Development Activities Focused on Technology Integration

Leaders can provide teachers with different opportunities to use technology tools to track the achievements of the students and the status of the attainment of learning goals. Leaders need to organize school level meetings and plan different training programs for the demonstration of these tools. Use a teacher-to-teacher model for the demonstration of these tools and give insights about how technology can be used to report the student's progress to parents and guardians.

Be an Advocate for Technology

Principals need to be knowledgeable about the national technology standards and must use these standards in their school. The leader should communicate the uses and the importance of technology to enhance student-learning experience to the stakeholders.

Benchmarking Other Schools

As new technologies are increasing, the schools need to anticipate and be prepared for the ongoing changes that take place. Leaders can exchange information with other schools that have a good reputation and benchmark.

Ways the Administrators, Teachers, and Students can Use Technology Effectively

School administrators have a lot of responsibilities to take care of in order to ensure proper functioning of the school. There are a number of tools available in the marketplace that can help the administrators with their tasks and help them succeed in it. These tools make the administrators more productive and efficient in their daily tasks. There are many ways where technology can enhance the productivity of administrators. To make the school administrators more productive, here is how technology should be incorporated.

- Administrators should make use of those technology tools that they want their teachers to be used within the classroom.

- They should be constant in their decisions to integrate technology in their school.

- They should clearly communicate with the communities of the school regarding the pace and process of technology integration.

- They need to provide proper professional development and resource to support the effective implementation of technology.

- They should make sure that the student's work is done and stored throughout these technologies.

- They should be active to support the students, staff, and the entire school in adopting the technology.

- They should use data gathering tools to have data present for decision-making.

- They should effectively communicate with teachers, students, parents, and the rest of the people associated with the school.

- They should encourage the use of web-based reports of student assessment results for school planning and professional development.

- They should assess students' information, manage it, and track students' progress.

- They should use electronic diagnostic tools in order to save time and measure the effectiveness of the lessons being taught in the school.

To be a successful administrator, you need to use several strategies to prepare yourself and your staff to understand the impact of these tools. School administrators can easily promote technology. They can encourage the teachers' curiosity about how to integrate technology in the everyday curriculum of students, provide incentives to teachers who attend relevant workshops and conferences, push teachers to use technology in their classroom as a model for others. Moreover, they should set up a mentoring system for the teachers to ask for help and ideas. The study conducted by the IT Trade Association CompTIA has proven that 75% of teachers and professors have admitted to the benefits of technology being incorporated in the classroom. Majority of the teachers have also confirmed that the use of innovative methods in education has proven to be helpful. Here are some examples:

- The internet has made it possible for humans to share the needed documents with anyone regardless of their location. With the help of portable devices, students have access to study materials whenever convenient to them. This means that the educational process is no longer limited to school hours.

- Technology has developed creativity and time management skills. The use of these new teaching methods has helped young people to be creative and work on exciting projects outside of the school and therefore, they also learn to acquire management skills.

- By comparing to a book, the weight of a tablet is much lesser. Therefore, students do not have to carry around heavy books. They can simply replace them with a portable device. This makes the process of learning more comfortable and simpler. And let's not forget that all the required data is stored in one place.

- Modern technology has saved numerous students' money. Young people and their parents spend tons of money every year buying new books for school, university or college. Nowadays, they spend money once to buy a good electronic gadget.

- With technology, students are more interested in gaining new knowledge. The old methods of teaching have outlived themselves a long time ago, and many students do not find them interesting. New innovations and technology have kept the students more engaged than they used to.

Technology in the digital era is changing and evolving by the literal minute. Educators need to keep up with innovations to prepare the students for this ever-changing world. We just witnessed how integrating technology with education has its benefits, but it is also important to note the traditional learning processes are still relevant in some circumstances.

There is growing evidence that technology integration leads to student achievement as well as improvement in academic performance. The Center for Applied Research in Educational Technology found that when technology is used as a learning method, leadership improves. Technology planning impacts achievement in learning content as well as it promotes a higher thought process and problem-solving skills. Technology also prepares students to be a part of the workforce. By incorporating technology into the education system, teachers and parents have a better view of the children's academic performances.

Students can easily draw a picture of the student's future based on their entire academic career. Teachers can detect when a student is not doing well and whether s/he needs help or not. This way, students become the prime concern of the teachers, and they can correct the students wherever applicable. Integrating technology in the classroom allows the school system to utilize the framework of personalized learning on a massive scale.

Chapter 12
Leadership Management /
Role of the Principal

"If school leadership were a true/false test, we could raise our scores by looking over the shoulder of an unsuccessful principal and choosing the opposite answer to each question."

-Todd Whitaker

Education has never been this important as it is today. It is high time to place leaders who are passionate about children and education in schools. School administrators or educational leaders need to realize the importance of ensuring if the educational system is operating effectively and efficiently. The leaders such as the principal, dean or headmaster demonstrate a high level of excellence in every field of education.

What is an Educational Leader?

In children's education and care services, the educational leader has an influential role to inspire, motivate, affirm, and challenge the practice of educators. The role is a collaborative journey that involves inquiry and reflection that has a significant impact on the important work that educators do.

Educational leadership is a collaboration of different talents and forces of teachers, students, and parents. Educational leadership is meant to improve the quality of education and the education system to make our children capable to face the real world.

The educational leader's purpose is to ensure that academics are succeeding through the process, material, and training improvements. This can be easily accomplished by collaborating with other individuals like other educators, parents of students, students, the policymakers and even the public. Thinking from a business perspective, educational leadership is a form of academic management and quality control.

Educational leaders play a vital role in affecting the attitude and reputation of the school. Educational leaders are the reason why students and teachers can function and grow. With a successful school leadership, schools are effective places where the students are challenged, educated, and encouraged.

An educational administrator is a specialized type of principal. Education administrators are employed in universities as well as colleges, schools, preschools, and even daycare centers. The conventional role of administrators is to make sure that all the schools, teachers, and counselors are collaborating and coordinating with a common goal as well as improving standards and opportunities.

The administration is responsible for the formation of curriculums, goals, budgets, timelines, state regulations, mandated testing, as well as performance measures that ensure all the educators to meet personal and professional goals. Administrators lead all the role players and lead the path to success for all.

School Principal as Leader

Traditionally, the principal played the role of the middle manager who would oversee all the functions in the school. However, in the recent era of rapidly changing standards, a new and different concept has emerged which suggests focusing on leadership with a clarity of what is essential and what needs to be done and how to get it done.

Principals can now no longer act just as building managers, having tasks that are meeting rules and carrying out those tasks and avoiding mistakes. Now, they have to be leaders of learning who has the capability to develop a team that delivers effective instruction.

As per The Wallace Foundation, there are five critical responsibilities of a principal:

- They create a vision that leads to academic success for all the students that is based on high standards.

- They create an environment that is hospitable so that a fruitful interaction is built.

- They enhance leadership in others so that the teachers and other individuals can play their part as per the school's vision.

- Principals improve the instructions given to the teachers so that they can teach at their level best while the students can learn them.

- They can manage people, data, and the processes for the improvement of the school.

Being an effective principal is not an easy job, and therefore, it is a long process. An effective principal is the one who is balanced within all their roles and works really hard to ensure that they are doing what is best for all the parties involved in the success of the school.

Successful principals know how to blend both of their roles as managers as well as leaders and carry out the tasks effortlessly. The best principals have a different mindset and possess the leadership philosophy that lets them be successful. They hold a combination of strategies that make them as well as the people around them better and successful.

Surrounded by Good Teachers

A principal's job becomes easier when they hire good teachers. Good teachers are strict disciplinarians, they deal with parents well and provide their students with the best education. This is what makes the principal's job easier. A principal is a person responsible for hiring the best teachers who are aware of what they are doing. As a principal who is devoted to the success of the school, it is best to be surrounded by good teachers who build the reputation of the school. This makes your job easier and allows you to easily manage other aspects of your job.

Take the Lead

A principal is the leader of the school. Every other person follows you as the principal and watches how you deal with the daily tasks. It is the responsibility of the principal to build a reputation for being a hard-worker in the institution. The rest of the employees will learn what they see. A principal becomes the model for fundamental qualities like equality, efficiency, and communication.

Be Creative

As a principal, pushing yourself to the limits is unfair to your position and your reputation. You need to be resourceful and find different and new ways to find solutions when critical situations arise. The principal is the one who encourages teachers to do the same as himself. As such, successful school principals are problem solvers.

Cooperative

As a principal, it is essential to learn to work with different types of people. A school has a number of people working in various positions and on various tasks. The best principals are those who are able to read and understand people well to figure out what demotivates and motivates them.

Dispositions and Characteristics of Effective Leaders

Dispositions are the inherent qualities of an individual. These are deeply rooted in every DNA. Some dispositions are helpful in being successful whereas, some of the dispositions can also have a negative impact on your leadership skills. Learning how to balance your positive and negative dispositions is what great leaders have. Enough practice and coaching can help make it easier to balance both aspects of these dispositions. Following are five dispositions that are found in successful school leaders.

Confidence

The first and most common disposition school leaders have is that the highly effective principals are very confident. The most effective leader is ambitious for the success of their organization, and the most effective school leader is focused on making decisions that are based on what is best for the student learning. School leaders are not afraid to make the decisions of what is best for the learning of the student. Highly effective principals have the confidence to lead regardless of the criticism they receive.

Risk Taker

Highly effective leaders are risk takers. This does not mean that they are careless and make senseless decisions, but it means that they operate from a prompt perspective. Great schools and organizations have leaders who learn by doing and are not afraid of failure.

Innovative

Highly effective leaders are innovative, creative and do things differently. They are focused on improving results and performances. They are innovative in leveraging time, talent, and resources to maximize human and social capital in the school to enhance student learning. They have the confidence to take risks and to think outside the box.

Assertive

Highly effective principals are aware of how to balance patience and persistence. They know how to view things from others' perspective and understanding the challenges, which are associated with change. Leaders are not afraid to move forward. They lead change and while doing so they praise those who are moving forward and continue to coach those people who are reluctant. Leaders who do not display empathy mostly end up sabotaging their own efforts.

Learner

To lead a learning organization, a school leader has to be a learner. Highly effective school leaders are updated through books, journals, newspapers, etc. They are active in their professional organizations and attend conferences and workshops. They study data of other schools and explore new strategies to help the school get better. These leaders share when they learn and put it to practice.

Sense of Humor

If a leader is innovative and takes risks, then having a great sense of humor is an advantage. With a great sense of humor, you can ease your tensions, resolve conflicts, increase positive interactions with others and reduce stress. Having a sense of humor allows leaders to have a positive impact on others and on themselves. A sense of humor is an attitude that leaders adopt so that they can find humor even in the most serious situations rather than being upset about everything.

Leaders also share positive characteristics along with these dispositions. To begin with a few characteristics, leaders are trustworthy, collaborative, great listeners, and caring. There is no single solution to becoming a successful leader and having a successful school leadership team. However, there are certain strategies, skills, traits, and beliefs that most of the leaders share.

They Understand the Importance of Building the Community

Effective school leaders build the community and maintain those partnerships to promote a caring and responsible school community. This is essential for effective leadership, and the best leaders are aware of it. In order to build these community networks, it is necessary that the leaders of the school are present in their schools and in their community, to develop trust and create a sense of transparency with the people associated with the school.

They Empower Teachers and Promote Leadership Skills

Great school leaders know that running a school is not a one-man show. They need to be surrounded by people and colleagues who are cooperative regarding the same vision. The leaders need to fully support the teachers and the staff by encouraging them to learn, develop, and help them become leaders themselves. Great principals focus on improving the quality of their teachers. They carefully hire the best teachers, support their efforts and their dreams and work with them carefully to support their development and the impact of student achievement.

They Use Data and Its Resources

Successful school leaders utilize data such as school-based assessments to maintain a continuous improvement for the purpose of promoting cultural opportunities for all the students. The opportunities that the data brings are what the effective leaders are able to control in order to make strategic decisions that benefit the students.

They Have a Plan and a Vision

The best leaders are also visionaries. They have a goal that they can use to unite a team and help them get there. They are also able to communicate the school's vision and goals.

Having a vision is one of the important qualities that a leader can possess because it is what provides a direction for himself and the team members. For leaders to be successful in their vision and plan, they need to have passion. Vision and passion together generate inspiration, motivation, and excitement that is spread throughout the school.

They Build a Collaborative Learning Environment

Inclusive learning provides the students with access to a very flexible learning choice and an effective path to achieve educational goals. The best educators are aware of this, and therefore inclusivity is their first priority. This creates a safe learning environment that can help and nurture the students. The leaders that prioritize inclusive learning believe that every person can be a part of the contribution to the greater learning community and encourage collaboration between the faculty and the students.

They are Passionate

Passion is critical for anyone who envisions success. However, passion is important for school leaders who create an influence on the school's culture.

Passionate people are contagious and can greatly affect the satisfaction of a teacher as well as the performance of a student.

They Promote Taking Risks

Educators are aware that failure is the greatest teacher of life. Effective leaders encourage taking risks among their staff. They create a supportive environment and reward with successful ideas and initiatives, regardless of the outcome. Similarly, teachers should also encourage their students to take risks to experience growth.

They Lead by Example

As mentioned earlier, dispositions can be positive or negative. Being a leader who takes the initiative and leads by example can be a trait as well as a characteristic. Leaders who lead by becoming the example and role models are not beneficial to students, but also to co-workers and parents. A leader who leads by example always gets respected and is admired.

They are Consistent

Change can be good; however, it can be harmful when it occurs too often. Talking about school leadership, it is recorded that frequent turnover creates a negative school environment, which negatively affects students' performance.

The best leaders commit to their school despite the obstacles or challenges that arise. Leaders are aware that true transformation takes time and a leader's commitment shows true passion and dedication, which has a positive effect on school culture.

They are Constant Learners

The most important quality a leader can have is the thirst for knowledge. The best leaders are those who know that they will never know enough. They are those who are humble in their knowledge and confident in their abilities. They are those individuals who are curious and never stop questioning and never stop learning.

"Leadership and learning are indispensable to each other"

-John F. Kennedy

Leadership Styles

As per the research conducted by Asaecenter, a leadership style is a way that a person uses his power to lead other people. The research has identified different kinds of leadership styles based on the number of followers. The most appropriate leadership style depends on the functionality of the leader, the followers, and the situation it was applied to. There are leaders who are not comfortable with the participation of many followers and some leaders do not have the ability to take up responsibility. Nevertheless, specific situations help identify the most effective styles of leadership. That being said, the following are 12 types of leadership styles that educational leaders can adopt in order to lead tomorrow's future.

Autocratic Leadership

This leadership style is centered on the boss. The leader in this leadership holds all the authority and responsibility. The leaders take all the decisions on their own without having the need to consult other subordinates. They take the decisions and communicate them to their subordinates. After which, they expect implementation and results.

This environment has very little or no flexibility at all. In this leadership, the guidelines, procedures, and policies are the autocratic leader's choice. When counted, there are a few instances that support autocratic leadership.

Democratic Leadership

Democratic leadership is also known as participative leadership or shared leadership. In this leadership style, the members of the group are asked to participate in making decisions. This leadership revolves around the idea that subordinates can contribute their ideas. A democratic leader holds the final decision; however, he represents authority to other people who work on the designated projects.

The most unique characteristic of this leadership is that communication takes place upward as well as downward. According to statistics, the Democratic leadership is the most preferred one as it displays fairness, creativity, competence, courage, honesty, and intelligence.

Strategic Leadership

Strategic leadership is where the leader is usually the head of the department. In strategic planning, executives that use different styles of management build a vision for their organization and enable their team members to adapt to it or be competitive in the changing market. Strategic leaders use this vision to motivate employees and departments, build a feeling of unity and direction to implement the change within their organization.

The strategic leader is the one who fills the gaps that come in between the need for a new possibility and the need for practical actions by giving a set of habits to adapt. 55% of this leadership requires a lot of strategic thinking.

Transformational Leadership

Transformational leadership is about bringing change in entities like organizations, groups or oneself. Transformational leadership inspires others to bring about positive changes in them. Transformational leaders motivate others to do more than they thought they could. They have high expectations and therefore, they achieve more.

Transformational leaders have a passionate, energetic, and enthusiastic approach. These leaders are not only concerned about the process, but they are also focused on helping each member of the group to succeed.

Research has proven that transformational leadership has more committed and satisfied followers. This is due to transformational leaders being able to empower their followers.

Team Leadership

Team leadership is all about working with the hearts and minds of the people involved. Team leadership is about recognizing that teamwork does not always involve trusting relationships. The hardest part of this leadership is predicting whether or not it will succeed. According to Harvard Business Review, team leadership fails due to poor leadership qualities.

Cross-Cultural Leadership

This form of leadership exists where there are a number of cultures in society. This leadership has grown in a way that it is used to recognize the front-runners who work in a globalized market. International organizations require leaders that can adjust their leadership effectively to work in different environments.

Facilitative Leadership

Facilitative leadership is dependent on the outcomes and not on skills. The effectiveness of a group is related to the effectiveness of its process. If a group is functioning well, the facilitative leader becomes less strict on the process. And if the group is not functioning up to the mark, the leader will be stricter in helping the group to progress. Effective facilitative leadership includes monitoring the group's dynamics, offering suggestions regarding the process and interventions to help keep the group on track.

Laissez-faire Leadership

Laissez-faire leadership is where the leader gives authority to his employees. The departments or subordinates are allowed to work as per their choice with minimal or no interference from the authorities. According to various findings, this kind of leadership is found to be the least satisfying and the least effective among all the management styles.

Transactional Leadership

This leadership is one that maintains the status quo. This leadership involves an exchange process where followers get immediate rewards for being obedient to the leader's orders. Transactional leadership has its focus on the exchange. Transactional leadership includes clarifying the performance of the followers that is expected, explaining how to meet those expectations and rewarding those on meeting the expectations.

Coaching Leadership

Coaching leadership involves the teaching and supervising of the followers. A coaching leader is one who is highly operational in deciding where improvement in performance is required. In this kind of leadership, followers are coached to improve their skills. Coaching leadership motivates, inspires, and encourages its followers.

Charismatic Leadership

It is the method of encouraging specific behaviors in others through constant communication, constant persuasion, and forcing of personality. Charismatic leaders motivate their followers to get the job done and improve the way they are doing certain things. They do this by developing eagerness in others for them to achieve their goal. The charismatic leadership is basically a form of heroism. This leadership style is of divine origin.

Visionary Leadership

Visionary leadership is a form of leadership that includes those leaders who are able to recognize the fact that methods, steps, and processes of leadership are attained through people. Great and successful leaders have the aspects of vision in them. Those who are visionaries are the ones who are considered to exhibit visionary leadership. Outstanding leaders are those who will always transform their visions into realities.

Chapter 13
Instructional and Curriculum Leader
What is Curriculum?

The term curriculum refers to the academic lessons and content that is being taught in school or in a specific course. As per the dictionaries, the curriculum is defined as the courses that are offered by an educational institution. However, it is seldom used in a general sense.

The curriculum typically refers to the knowledge and skills that the students are expected to learn. This includes learning standards or learning objectives that they are likely to meet, the different lessons that the teachers teach, the assignments given to the students, the books, presentations, reading materials, tests, assessments and other methods that are used to evaluate the learning of students.

In most of the cases, teachers build their own curricula. They refine them and improve them over the years. It is a common practice for teachers to adapt lessons that have been created by other teachers, use the same curriculum templates as guides to structure their own lessons or even purchase curricula from individuals or even companies. There are certain scenarios where the schools purchase complete and multi-grade curriculum packages that the teachers are instructed to use.

Types of Curriculum

The curriculum reflects the models of instruction. Therefore, people may categorize the curriculum according to common psychological classifications of the four learning theories.

Written Curriculum

This is the written part of an instruction of schooling. It may include documents relating to the curriculum, films, texts and any supporting materials that are chosen to support the agenda of the school. Therefore, the curriculum matches the written understandings and directions that are designed and reviewed by the administrators, directors, and teachers.

Societal Curriculum

This is the type of curricula that can be expanded to include the most powerful effects of social media. This curriculum takes a look at how it actively helps create new perspectives and therefore, can help shape the student accordingly so that he can be accepted within the society.

The Hidden Curriculum

It refers to the lessons that are unwritten, unofficial, and unintended that students learn in school. The formal curriculum consists of courses, lessons, and activities for students to participate in. On the other hand, the hidden curriculum includes of academic, social, and cultural messages that are unspoken to the students while they are in school.

This concept revolves around the recognition that students learn lessons in school that are or are not a part of their formal study. For example, how they are supposed to interact with peers, teachers and other adults, how they should perceive different ethnic groups or what ideas and behaviors are acceptable and unacceptable.

The Null Curriculum

The null curriculum refers to a situation where the students do not have the opportunity to learn. The students are learning something without specific experiences, interactions, and courses in the classroom.

For example, if the students are not taught to question, they are learning something that may not be useful to them. Simply put, what is not included in the curriculum can be present in what the students are learning.

Concomitant Curriculum

It is the curriculum that is taught at home, or the experiences that are a part of a family, or other related experiences that are approved by the family. These include teachings received at church, ethics, behaviors or social experiences.

Rhetorical Curriculum

The elements of the rhetorical curriculum are comprised of ideas offered by policymakers, school officials, administrators or even politicians. The curriculum can be derived from professionals that are involved in the formation of content, or from those educational steps that have been taken based on national and state reports, public speeches etc.

Curriculum-in-use

Sometimes, the formal curriculum is not frequently taught to the students. The curriculum-in-use refers to the actual curriculum that is being taught by the teacher to the students.

Received Curriculum

This is referred to the curriculum that the students have actually learned and taken out of the classrooms. The concepts that they have truly learned and remembered are the received curriculum.

The Internal Curriculum

The internal curriculum comprises the processes, content, and knowledge combined with the experiences and realities of the learners. Each student has a different understanding and educators have the option to explore this curriculum by using different instructional assessments to see what students remember from a lesson.

The Electronic Curriculum

Any lesson that is learned from the internet or through different e-forms is known as electronic curriculum. This type of curriculum can be classified as formal or informal, good or bad, correct or incorrect depending on one's understanding and views.

Students who use the internet on a regular basis for recreation or for personal use face a number of messages on all types of media and messages. They may be correct and informative, or they may be manipulative as well.

Importance of Curriculum

The curriculum is a criterion that is used to provide experiences to the learners so that they can reach the maximum growth of their personalities. Education has the same role. However, without a curriculum, education is pointless. Various reasons as to why the curriculum is important are listed as follow:

Development of Individuals

Every individual has his own set of abilities, knowledge, interests, talents, skills, and understandings. All learners do not understand on the same pace and do not learn the same. However, the curriculum can create opportunities for learners to learn at their own pace.

A proper curriculum set can help the students by providing them with such experiences that will help the students mentally.

The curriculum consists of curricular and co-curricular activities. Thus, it plays an essential role in mental, social, emotional, and physical development. The curricular activities help with the spiritual growth whereas, co-curricular activities help in the development of the learner's personalities.

Develops Basic Skills

A curriculum helps with building basic skills such as reading, speaking, writing, and understanding. When a suitable curriculum is applied, the learner's skills are enhanced to be used in the best suitable situation.

Preserves Cultural Heritage

The curriculum of education can be used to preserve a society's culture and transmit it to the next generation. It preserves culture in areas like literature and art with the help of a proper teaching-learning process.

Used for Betterment of People

The curriculum can help in making people think openly. Different aspects of life are taught which help broaden the mind and accept the realities of life. It helps in developing attitudes of people towards life. A proper curriculum, when taught well to the learner, helps enhance his knowledge about facts around the world. Thus, with this curriculum, these learners grow up to be scientists, educationists or people specialized in their fields.

Instructional Leadership

Instructional leadership in education has its focus on learning for children as well as adults. It focuses on the learning that can further be measured by the development of instructions and the learning of the student. For instructional leadership to be effective, there needs to be a culture of practice in the school community. Instructional leaders focus on managing individuals and resources effectively. Either a manager or a school administrator takes the role of instructional leadership. Principals who give instructional leadership do not get too occupied in dealing with administrative duties. They play the role that involves setting clear goals, managing the curriculum, evaluating teachers, monitoring lesson plans, and assigning resources to instructions.

There are four skills that have been identified as essential for effective instructional leadership in principals.

Effective Use of Resources

It is not enough for principals to only know about their faculty's strengths and weaknesses. If there are specific resources that can benefit the staff, then the principal should be ready to provide them. Principals need to recognize that their teachers work hard to be appreciated so their performance should be considered when allocating resources.

Communication Skills

Instructional principals need to be excellent communicators. Interpersonal skills are vital for the success of a principal. They need to be able to communicate their beliefs in regard to education. These skills build trust, build motivation, and empower teachers as well as students.

Serve as an Instructional Resource

Teachers depend on the principals as well as other higher authorities to have enough sources of information that are related to instructional practices. Instructional leaders need to be updated with all of the issues and current events that arise related to curriculum and effective student assessment.

Being Visible and Accessible

Good principals have a positive and vibrant presence in the school. They need to model learning behaviors, focus on learning objective and lead by example. Aside from these qualities, a successful instructional principal must have good planning and observation skills to evaluate the performances of the staff as well as the students.

The role of the instructional leader should not be limited and must always keep evolving. Their role should be more than just managing or conducting administrative tasks. They should focus on leadership. To achieve this objective, a principal having solid ideas is not enough. Success requires redefining the role of the principal.

The role of the principal as an instructional leader is described as one that needs to focus on building a learner's community. It requires making a shared decision and getting back to basics. It requires management of time, support of professional development for the staff, creating an environment of integrity, and using resources to support an educational game plan. Moreover, they should have room for improvement.

For principals to really succeed in being an instructional leader, they should work hard to free themselves from the teaching rituals. When the instructional methods are implemented successfully, you will be able to allow students as well as teachers to build and maintain a meaningful environment for learning.

Vision for Learning

What does it mean to be an educated person? Educators who have been raised and educated in the 20th century tend to approach the image of an educated person from a less current perspective. However, it is important that we look at what an educated person is as per the 21st century.

In the early years, the purpose of the school was to prepare learners to be able to live within a society and abide by the values and norms that come with it. A member of the society had a maintained job, which meant providing a service, which was financially compensated. It was a usual practice when an employee would work for the same company for their entire life, doing the same job until they retired.

These jobs did not need much, only a little knowledge and skill that was received in high school or college. The education system back then did a good job of providing workers with a suitable job. However, this is not the case in the 21st century.

The 21st century brought along with it new scopes of jobs and opportunities for workforce development such as e-business, nanotechnology, and homeland security that had never existed in the previous century. If the educational system was still the same as it was back then, in that case, the employees would not be compatible with the job description. With the pace of change in employment, it is quite clear that acquiring the knowledge and skills for only a specific type of job is not enough. An educated person of the 21st century has to be adaptable, flexible, and full of knowledge to be able to switch between jobs and careers. Being productive requires flexibility and the ability to rebuild when needed. Therefore, the educational system needs to be updated.

The 21st-century education system has been defined as a model that focuses more on the academic content as well as the set of skills that is needed to function in this digital world. The new skill sets include innovation and creativity, critical thinking, problem-solving, communication, collaboration, flexibility, adaptability, social skills, leadership, and responsibility.

The instructional approach includes the needed 21st-century skills with the academic content that is being taught to students. With this approach, teachers will become more engaged with their students. Engaged learners are successful learners.

The education system should be able to provide the learners with the skills and knowledge that will be needed in order for them to be called an educated person. This can be done by guiding the learners to design who they are, discover their strengths, and develop the person as a whole. The shift in paradigm takes place when each learner is provided with the ability to know who they are instead of telling them who they are and what they need to be.

Community of Leadership

While building a community of leadership, the leaders need to focus on smoothing the process of familiarizing people with each other. Research shows that people trust others very seldom. This is because the leaders of our society are losing their sense of community.

How can leaders address this matter? They can start by making time and getting to know each other and increasing interactions. Leaders are those who build relationships by building a physical space where people can interact. Moreover, leaders should pay attention to the environment where the employees work.

Most of the times, organizational leaders focus their recruitment on the usual norm of managerial skills and professional experiences. Leaders look for skills that are technical and intellectual in nature and therefore, they fail to find the skills that are needed to engage and lead diverse communities. This causes leaders to overlook the less conventional skills that are offered by the community residents.

The reality is that the skills that are less conventional are key to successful leadership. The shift between the qualifications of professional managers and those that the community has to offer discourages the ability of organizations to make a meaningful and long-lasting change of system in their communities.

By redefining the skills needed for leadership and success in the organization, community members bring creativity, networks, perspectives, and social capital that become assets to the progression of an organization. This opens up possibilities for leaders who have a number of capabilities that become valuable and important regarding the effectiveness of an organization.

Redefining the skillsets results in a better performance on the community's part because the evaluation of performance is aligned with the employee's strengths instead of evaluating the skills that they haven't learned. This tactic helps the people in a community to be partners with each other, and such a partnership is an essential ingredient when creating a meaningful change in places where people have been under-valued for a long time.

When an organization becomes partners with the whole community and embraces the resources, capacities, and the talents that exist within the community, it is imperative to create a real and lasting social change.

Teacher Leadership

The term 'teacher leadership' is related to a set of skills that is demonstrated by teachers who not only teach students but have an influence outside the classroom as well. In other words, it means mobilizing and energizing others with the goal of improving the performance of the school's responsibilities which is related to teaching and learning. Mobilizing and energizing students do not necessarily take place due to the role of the leader, but they also occur due to the individual being informed and persuasive. Therefore, an important characteristic of a teacher being a leader is the skill he has while engaging others in complex work. It also requires passion to fulfill the mission of the school and the courage to face the obstacles that arise when achieving that mission. The improvement of a school's performance involves doing things differently than how they have been done in the past. Teacher leadership requires a process of change. However, this is not always the case.

Most of the times, improvement takes place when teachers motivate their colleagues to be more skilled and thoughtful in their work as well as when they encourage them to do things better than before. At other times, teachers who act as a leader tend to identify an opportunity to incorporate such a practice, which could improve the program of the school. In those situations, teacher leadership does not require using a new approach; however, the change process that is involved does not mean the implementation of a new program. Rather, it is a professional exploration of practice.

Professional Learning Communities

The idea of the improvement of schools through development or professional learning communities is currently trending. People use this term to describe every combination imaginable, which is highly linked to education, such as, a school committee, a school district, a high school department, state department of education, a grade level teaching team, etc.

The professional learning community model has reached a critical phase where the fate of other well-intentioned school efforts has been witnessed. A professional learning community is known as a group of educators who have regular meetings, share expertise, and work collaboratively to improve the teaching skills and the performances of the students. The term is also used in schools or faculty members who use a small group for professional development.

Professional learning communities serve two purposes; firstly, to improve the skills and knowledge of the teachers through extensive study, exchange of expertise, and professional use of dialogue. The second purpose is achieved by improving the educational achievements, aspirations as well as the attainment of students through strong leadership and teaching.

Chapter 14
Developing and Sustaining Community Engagement

When schools work on strengthening relationships with families and with the organizations of the community, they get into an environment that has a great impact on students. There are a number of definitions of community engagement; however, in its simplest form, community engagement focuses on integrating the community with the students in a way to achieve constant long-term outcomes, processes, relationships, discourse, decision-making and even implementation.

Engagement is not driven by a framework of guiding principles. The framework of engagement is based on various principles that enlighten the *right* of all the community members to be informed, consulted, involved, and empowered. Community engagements include a range of tools and strategies to ensure that success is achieved. The word "community" is a term that is used to define the different groups of people that include stakeholders, interest groups, businesses and citizen groups. A community can be formed on the basis of a geographic location, similar interest or affiliation (such as a sporting club, snooker club, etc.). Therefore, community engagement is a strategic process that has a specific purpose of working with these groups of people who are connected through geographic location, interest or even identity. Moreover, community engagement deals with issues that affect the community's well-being.

Creating a link between "community" and "engagement" broadens the scope of education and therefore, the focus shifts from the individual to a collective group along with the associated implications for inclusiveness to ensure diversity exists within the community.

Why Community Engagement?

A recent study regarding community engagement has identified different areas where the community engagement has had an impact on. Although this study focused on the partnerships of research, many of its findings were relevant to community engagement.

Agenda

Engagement of the community changes the choice of projects, how these projects are initiated, and the potential to gain funds through these projects. New areas for collaboration are found, and funds that need community engagement become accessible.

Design and Delivery

The improvements used to study design, tools, interventions, participation, data collection and analysis, communication and dissemination can be executed. New ideas can be identified through the knowledge of the community. The speed and efficiency of the project can be improved by engaging the partners and the participants as well as by looking for new sources of information.

Implementation and Change

Improvements can be achieved in a way where research findings are used to bring change and create capacity for change and maintain long-term relationships.

Ethics

Community engagement builds opportunities to improve the consent process, look for ethical pitfalls, and create the process for resolving the ethical problems when they arise.

People Involved in the Project

The knowledge of the public that is involved in the project can be improved, and their contributions can be recognized. These efforts bring goodwill and therefore, can help lay the groundwork for collaborations.

Understanding the Importance of Engaging All Stakeholders

Engaging with stakeholders is necessary for the success of any organization. For an organization to succeed, the organization needs to have a clear vision that is derived from a strategic planning process and have an effective plan that is derived through stakeholder engagement.

Effective engagement helps in converting the needs of the stakeholders into organizational goals and creates the basis of effective strategy development. When you discover the point of consensus, it helps the group of stakeholders to arrive at a decision and guarantee that an investment has a fruitful outcome. Without any internal alignment, there cannot be an effective strategy. Stakeholders differ depending on the organization. Stakeholders may include employees, suppliers, customers, shareholders, government agencies, business owners, and board of directors. Each of the stakeholders has a unique vision of what it takes for the organization to succeed.

A shared understanding is necessary when building a vision for the future. We bring value to the strategic and marketing plans by implementing a process of engagement and providing a forum for discussion.

Involve stakeholders when evaluating, planning and implementing, and adding value by:

- Providing new perspectives on what is credible, high quality and of useful evaluation

- Contributing to the logic of a program and framing the key evaluating question

- Helping in the collection of quality data

- Making sense of the data that has been collected

- Increasing the utilization of the findings in the evaluation by building knowledge and support for the evaluation.

Benefits of School-Community Partnerships
Bringing the Real World into the Classroom

It is important for students to see the things they are learning implemented in real life. Business owners and people who are specialized in certain areas can help give students real-life examples of how they will be using subjects like science, math, writing, reading and creative skills in their future working lives.

Improve Understanding

When different business owners and local community members come together in a classroom, students get the opportunity to meet people that they might not know otherwise. Business owners also get the chance to see the environment of their local schools.

Encourage Creativity

Jobs are always changing and evolving with time. Many jobs today exist that were not available a few years ago.

These are those jobs that students are not aware of. By inviting the community into the classroom, students can discover job opportunities that they were not aware of. This helps in the formation of the future of the students.

Strengthen Programs

Teachers can learn from experts in the community. People put their knowledge into practice and understand recent trends. By partnering with the community, teachers can strengthen the curriculum that can help enhance the understanding of the students. In return, businesses can learn about the activities and the lessons that work well on specific topics. They can also improve their professional development and training based on teaching skills that they will learn in the classroom.

Examples of Ways to Engage the Community

There are great examples of school partnerships. These help to ensure a healthy contribution to the needs of 21st-century learners. In order to uplift schools into a position that suits the 21st-century learners, the community needs to help regarding it.

Schools usually focus on the day-to-day academic and social events, but it is vital that school leaders make time for the extended community. These citizens help in the school's overall support. Looking for ways to engage with the community is necessary especially if you are looking for ways to significantly bring changes to your school.

Organize an Open House and Curriculum Fair

Build a unique opportunity for the community to look for high-quality work that your school is providing through a curriculum fair or an open house. Instead of shutting yourself away from the public, you need to develop a strong connection with your community by demonstrating the good deeds of your school. Teachers need to demonstrate their best work and prepare themselves to speak about the goals and objectives of the school.

Engage with Civic Groups

Make sure to engage with the different civic organizations such as Boy Scouts, local business clubs, and recreational sports leagues in the district. By developing different partnerships with these groups, one can help build the cultural role of the school in the community.

Attend Non-school Events

Attending a non-school event gives the message that you care for the entire community and not just your school. This helps you engage with citizens with informal conversations and therefore, sets a positive image for the future. Non-school sports games, civic events, community art exhibitions, and showcases are examples of non-school events.

Use Social Media to Create Engagement

Social media is a new era. Sharing information with the community on a website is not a substitute for engaging with the community. Social media should be where people are redirected to opportunities for in-person engagement.

Schools are required by society to combine traditional and new strategies to keep everyone engaged and interested in the school. The community expects the school to be accountable and transparent. Therefore, this makes it clear that the school plays an active role in the establishment of the public perspective of the school itself. These strategies help spread a good word about the culture of the school.

Scenarios about community engagement

The benefits of building community and community engagement are countless. Community engagement brings in more leads and increases brand loyalty as well as user retention. The community engagement strategy is a process of building your customers. It is essential to understand that there are a number of communities and each of which has its own values and interests. Therefore, in most of the cases, there is not a single solution to community engagement. Volunteering is one of the best ways to encourage community involvement in schools. Schools can connect with local businesses, charity organizations, civic organizations, nonprofit foundations and other groups in the community for volunteers.

Schools can invite local leaders from the community to visit different classes and speak about different professions for Career Day. Community members can be encouraged to get involved with the school in activities like tutoring, fine arts, and even athletic teams. Not every organization, family, individual or even business in your community has the time to participate in all volunteering opportunities, which is why it is important to prioritize the involvement of the community in the form of sponsors or donations.

The responsibility of raising a well-educated and civic-minded child cannot solely depend on the school. Studies have shown a positive relationship between family involvement and benefits for the students. This chapter discusses the role of the community's engagement with the school in historical, empirical, and theoretical aspects. The community plays a substitute, critical, and complementary role in the development of education. Moreover, the role of the community and its impacts change on the basis of country, region, etc.

The participation of the community in school management has a great potential in removing mistrust and distances between people and the schools by making the information transparent and developing a culture of mutual respect. In those countries where the administration is weak, the approach of expanding the educational opportunity may be the only option. However, when the community is involved, the results are overwhelming.

The involvement of the community in education enhances the resources for education as well as it takes part in defining educational programs throughout the community.

- Parents can work with teachers to guide students

- Community organizations can encourage all the potential learners to participate in learning activities

- Communities can also help the learning activities to work in a mutually supportive way.

- Schools and universities can recognize funds and acknowledge the value of them. These funds can be availed within the family as well as the community.

By introducing the community into the classroom, everyone involved in the school stakeholder list benefits from it. Students learn from people who have already experienced the real world. As a result, the students are exposed to jobs that they were never aware that existed. Teachers help make the lessons more engaging and authentic. The schools gain the support of the community and therefore, the businesses get more involved in the community, which helps them gain more clients.

Chapter 15
Safety and School Culture

As a school leader, the top and foremost commitment is to improve the learning of the student. In order to achieve it, you need to refine instructional practice among your staff. However, before going into the process of sifting through data and increasing the school's standards, you need to know that creating a positive school culture has a huge impact on the success of the school.

Why is school culture so important? One major reason is that it defines character and sets a standard for behavior. Your kids spend about one-third of their lives in a place that builds their character. You would not want them to be in a place with a devoid culture or a place with negative cultural values. They might end up developing socially inappropriate behaviors if they stay in that culture for too long.

A social psychologist R.S. Barth says, *"A school culture has a more powerful influence on life and learning in the schoolhouse as compared to the state of department of education, the superintendent, the school board, or even the principal can ever have."* One of his peers, Nancy Watson also added, *"If the culture is not welcoming to the student, achievement cannot be acquired."*

Studies have proven that the academic schools that have been highly rated also have a positive culture that contributes to academic achievement. Schools as such not only value their culture but they also expect it. For them, it is a standard that needs to be achieved because it is a cultural value.

It has been proven that if a school community such as the teachers, administrators, parents, and support staff all have the same value for academic achievement, then students will eventually follow the same footsteps. Similarly, if the school and its members do not value culture and do not expect a high academic achievement, then none of the students will strive to learn.

In short, a school's culture is what can make or break the educational experience of the child. Therefore, it is necessary to ensure that children have a good experience at school.

Safety and Crisis Plans

A situation or an event that causes psychological trauma to the students and the staff, which requires prompt action due to the potential of disruption caused to the educational process, is known as a school crisis. It has the ability to impact a small group of students in a classroom and even the entire school community.

A school crisis may include the death of a student or a staff member, suicide attempt of a student or a staff member, natural disasters such as earthquake, volcano, etc. or any other mishaps.

Forming a crisis management plan is quite a task for the school's management as they are never sure where to begin. Following a number of steps can help manage the process and help you take actions. There are four phases of crisis management: Mitigation, Preparedness, Response, and Recovery. Each of these steps are designed to encourage thoughts about crisis preparedness. To break it down easier, there are four phases of crisis management:

- Mitigation is what the schools can do to reduce the risk to life and property.

- Preparedness focuses on what to expect.

- Responses are the steps that the responsible ones take when a crisis event occurs.

- Recovery is the act of restoring the environment back to normal after a crisis event takes place.

Mitigation

You can never prevent a crisis from happening, but you can act to decrease the effects of certain events and reduce the damage that the crisis can cause. To be prepared for a crisis, the officials need to assess their campus and calculate the amount of risk that can damage the campus. Taking steps accordingly can reduce the damage caused by the crisis.

Preparedness

Planning for a crisis takes a lot of time and resources however, it is necessary to have a prompt and effective response. You need to be realistic regarding the time for which you need to have a proper crisis plan, as well as you need to define the roles and responsibilities of each staff member of the school.

Response

How you respond to a crisis is crucial. You need to identify the type of crisis that has occurred and try your best to react instantly. Notify the relevant authorities and try your best to evacuate the campus. Keep all the necessary supplies nearby and provide first aid to those who are in need. Lastly, you need to track each and every action taken and record all the damages and the expenditures for further insurance purposes.

Recovery

Recovery is the process where you restore the environment for it to be conducive to a safe learning place. The staff members are trained to evaluate the emotional needs of the students as well as the school members; they are also able to provide support and to build a comfortable environment within the campus.

School Climate

School climate is a widely used term. In the early days, the use of school climate denoted the ethos or the spirit of an organization. Nowadays, the school climate is used to represent the attitude presented by the school. The mood or morale of a certain group is how people are perceived. If a teacher is happy, s/he is considered to be a better teacher.

As mentioned earlier, students spend a significant portion of their time at schools. And the way students feel about their schools can have a big impact on their daily lives. Students need to feel safe at school, but they also need to feel comfortable in their environment.

A positive school climate has been linked to a positive development in the student's learning, academic achievement, health promotion, low dropout rates, teacher retention, academic achievement, high graduation rates, etc.

School Climate vs School Culture?

There is no clear definition that defines a school climate, however, school climate is defined as the *"quality and character of school life"*. According to the School Climate Council, the school climate must involve the experiences of learning and relationship building of the individuals in the school, as well as it should capture the beliefs and attitudes present in the school. School climate is more than just about the experience of an individual, it is an overall experience of the school. On the other hand, school culture is also defined as the values, beliefs, teaching patterns, rules, behaviors, and learning approaches that are shared among the individuals in the school. The school culture includes a school's norms, traditions, rules, and expectations. These affect the way how people dress, how they interact with others, and how they act with certain people.

Comparing School Climate & Culture

School culture is mostly used in exchange with school climate, but the school climate is referred to the experience of the individual and the feelings of students and the staff regarding the school. On the other hand, school culture refers to the long-term physical and social environment and the beliefs that are shared between individuals of the school.

Climate can also be categorized as the *"attitude"* or *"mood"* of the school, while culture is the *"personality"* or *"values"* of the school. Climate is perception-based, whereas values and beliefs shape culture. To make it simpler, the climate is how people physically feel in the school whereas, culture is how people act in school.

Both school climate and school culture are important when understanding the environment of the school and studying the experiences of the students. This is a building block of school culture.

Assessing your School Climate

There are a number of school surveys that are available in recent times. These are used to measure different factors from mental health and bullying to drug use and more. One popular measurement used today is called the school climate survey.

School climate surveys are measures that assess different aspects of the educational environment to be aware of the strengths and weaknesses of a school. The goal of these measures is to have a true image of the school so that they can further improve the areas that are lacking.

School climate measures many different features of the school environment depending on the goals of the school. Some of the factors include:

- School safety

- Leadership of the school

- Students and their learning

- Teaching experiences

- Needs for training

- Decision-making process

- Careers and intentions

Research has found that having a positive school climate helps solve many problems like bullying, disengaged students, cultural and socio-economic differences, vandalism, teacher burnout, etc. Studies have proven that a positive school climate can reduce the number of absenteeism, substance abuse, suspensions and bullying as well as it can help increase the academic achievement of students, their motivation to learn, and their psychological well-being.

It can also alleviate the negativity of socio-economic status and self-criticism. Also, working in a positive climate prevents the teachers from being burned out, while simultaneously increasing teachers' retention rates. However, creating a positive school climate is not an easy job. People have a mind of their own and therefore, it is not easy to make them feel optimistic as you please. It takes a lot to implement before the school climate is maintained. What is it like to have a positive school climate? When you walk into the campus, you can sense the positive school climate by the interactions that people have with each other and how the school's environment is.

You can notice the climate by how happy the teachers, students, and the school's management seem to be. Another factor to notice the school's climate is by evaluating how the staff members are treating each other. Is the school clean and is everything organized? Notice the bulletin boards whether they are maintained. These are the physical factors through which you can have an idea about the school's climate.

The National School Climate Council, in 2007, enlisted the factors that define a positive school climate:

- People respect each other, and they engage with each other.

- Students, teachers, and family members help each other build a shared vision of the school.

- Each and every person in the school contributes to the actions of the school and cares about the environment of the school.

- The school has norms, values, and expectations that further support the social, physical, and emotional safety of the school.

- The educators develop the attitudes that focus on the benefits of learning.

- Strategies for improving school culture and climate.

Strategies for Improving School Culture and Climate

Before anything else, relationships come first. Building a positive environment in the classrooms and throughout the school is a step toward maintaining relationships. It requires commitment and stability from each member of the team such as administrators, support staff, and teachers to create a stable environment within the school.

As per the Boys Town Education Model, here are a few simple ways to improve your school's culture:

Build Relationships that are Strong

Managing a school soundly depends on the quality of relationships that teachers form with their students. The staff and student relationship affect the social climate of the school as well as the individual performance of the students. When the students are liked and appreciated by their teachers, they feel successful academically and mentally. On the contrary, if the students sense a weak relationship with their teacher, they lose their trust in the teacher and therefore, fear and failure start taking over the school culture.

It should be the first priority of the school to build a strong relationship. Teachers need to take time out and talk to their students out of the classrooms and maintain positive interaction with the students. To understand their students, teachers need to take interest in the students' lives outside of school, learn about their goals, their activities, and their struggles in life.

Teach Social Skills

The teachers and the school's management need to facilitate the students to learn how to listen to others and communicate in a respectful manner. They need to teach students how to argue positively. The students need to learn the appropriate social and emotional behaviors.

These behaviors include honesty, concern, respect to others, sensitivity, reliability, sense of humor, etc. As a staff member of the school, you need to look for the positive social skills that you would want to find in your students.

Get on the Same Page with Your Students

Every classroom has a different kind of environment, and each of those environments contribute to the culture of the school. Sometimes the adults are required to change in order to bring the change in students. Therefore, as a staff, you need to have a shared vision of the school.

This means that you need to develop rules to define and match with student behaviors. When the students come to believe that the rules are fair, it builds trust in them. Students need to know that bad behavior comes with consequences and will not be tolerated.

Become Role Models

Students are known to learn by watching just like learning by doing. They observe the actions of the influencers such as teachers, coaches, and facilitators, how they respond to situations and how they cope with unfamiliar situations. You need to keep a check on what messages your staff is communicating with the students.

For example, when a student is rejected by his peers, the rejection will stop if the teacher shows friendly behavior towards the student. Being educators, you are the ones who will set the example.

Implement Classroom and School Rules

Positive rules build a stable environment that can further lead to healthy interactions. Classroom rules are easy and simple to follow. For example, being respectful and talking with kindness can be easily followed by the students. You do not need to have a rule about chewing gum in class or asking permission to drink water. These issues do not lead to good behavior. Rules also need to be consistent. The same should be expected from the student in the classroom, the gym, and the cafeteria.

Teach Problem Solving

Problems are inevitable. Students have the ability to recognize a problem and solve them as long as we teach them how to. Teachers need to be open to listen to the problems that students face and be able to train them to solve their problems accordingly. Problem-solving can be used to help the students in making positive decisions in the future.

Have Specific Consequences

It is crucial to have classroom and school-wide rules to bring a structure to your school. However, students will still push the limits and go against them. This is when they need to face the consequences if they do so. Effective consequences give an understanding to the students that there is a direct connection with what they do and what happens after they committed such act. Consequences need to be effective immediately and have to be consistent among all students. Most importantly, these consequences need to be delivered with empathy and not with anger.

Praise Your Students for Good Choices

Many of the students do not receive enough positive feedback, both in the classroom as well as in their personal lives. When students are appropriately appraised, they tend to do better in life. Generalized comments like *"Good Job!"* are not enough. It would help if you were specific when praising a student, as doing so can help reinforce a behavior.

Three Steps to a Positive Climate

There is no specific formula to build a positive school climate. It mostly depends on the values and vision of the leaders and how everyone else agrees to them. It all begins with trust because it is a prerequisite to creating a positive climate.

Research has suggested some steps for school leaders to follow when cultivating positive school climate:

Assess the Climate

Before taking further steps, you need to know where you currently stand. You can revert to your staff and ask them for suggestions to create a positive school climate. This will also give a positive feeling to the teachers that they are being heard. Make sure to include everyone's opinions.

There are a number of ways to assess the climate of your school, two of which have been mentioned earlier in the chapter. Another way to know about the school's climate is by conducting one-on-one interviews with the school staff to ensure honesty.

Build a Shared Vision

Research proves that by bringing people together to brainstorm, a shared vision will build the kind of climate that they are looking for. However, according to Peter Senge, the Director of the Society for Organizational Learning, a shared vision must include personal visions of the staff. This way, people will be committed to the shared vision as a part of it will contain their visions too.

Before creating a vision that is shared among all, ask each and every member to write down his or her personal vision. Incorporate those visions to make a collective vision that everyone will work to achieve.

Work Together to Achieve the Shared Vision

To create a positive school climate, you should bring everyone together so that they can collectively work together toward a common goal. It may seem like a lot of work however, working together will ensure interaction among the peers and will make it fun when achieving the goal. A positive school climate will bring joy and fun into teaching and learning for the students.

Chapter 16
Ethics and Law

Ethics refer to the well-defined standards that claim any action to be right or wrong. Ethics help differentiate between values such as integrity, discipline, and honesty and how they are applied in daily lives. Ethics are what influence the behavior and therefore, allow an individual to make the right decisions. The importance of ethics cannot be ignored in life and therefore, they are acted upon even in the field of education.

Ethics in education are necessary as they help run the educational system smoothly. It sets the standards of what is acceptable and what is not appropriate in the field of education while protecting the interests of the educators and the students.

Ethics in education have been given a lot of importance since the past few years, which is why different institutions are creating courses to help the students understand ethics in education. These ethics are applicable to both educators and learners.

Teachers play a significant role in a student's life. Not only do they deliver education to the students, but they also help in building the personality of the student. The teachers are the instructors, and therefore they play the role of a mentor. They influence the development of an individual, and so it is crucial that they follow certain ethics.

The Student-Teacher Relationship

In Pennsylvania, attendance of students in school has been made mandatory and therefore, parents are left with no choice but to trust the education system. As a result, trust has become the foundation of the relationship of students with their teachers. Due to this foundation, it is the duty of the teachers to act as a trustable figure for the best interest of their students and to create and maintain a safe environment for the students.

As per the Code of Professional Practice and Conduct for Educators, *"Professional educators shall exert reasonable effort to protect the students from conditions, which interfere with learning or are harmful to the student's health and safety."*

The majority of facilitators in Pennsylvania commit to their responsibilities with care and conviction. However, there are a few who breach their duties and weaken the profession as an educator and as a result, lead this profession toward devastation, especially in cases where students are involved as victims. About 60-70% of the cases of the PSPC involve some type of sexual misconduct that includes criminal cases of sexual offenses, violation of boundaries with students, and abusive use of school equipment like accessing sexually explicit materials on the school computers. When a teacher enters into an inappropriate relationship with a student, the teacher breaches the boundaries of a student and teacher relationship, and therefore redefines the boundaries but rather inappropriately.

Some teachers groom a student intentionally so that they can engage in sexual misconduct, whereas other students fall prey to misconduct. For example, the relationship between the teacher and the student may start appropriately, and at some point, during the relationship, it takes a turn where the student serves the teacher instead of the teacher helping the student. Such a relationship may have a more physical interaction, which may lead to a sexual relationship. When teachers play the role of being friends or confidants of the students, a dual relationship is built which creates vagueness in the relationship and therefore, the roles are redefined. This uncertainty leads to inappropriate actions and misconduct.

It is necessary for all teachers to protect the well-being of the students inside and outside of school. Teachers must not put their needs before the students, but they must work to ensure that their colleagues follow the appropriate standards of ethical conduct.

Types of Student-Teacher Relationships

Majority of the teachers are trustworthy and work under a proper moral compass. They work professionally and take their job very seriously. They set high standards for their students as well as for themselves. These are the teachers that would never compromise the trust of their students, parents, school, and administrators.

However, there is a small but growing group of teachers from both the genders that engage with students with the intentions of having inappropriate relationships with them. As a consequence of committing such an act, they pay a high price once caught. The first type of a negative relationship between the student and the teacher is initiated by young, inexperienced, and immature teachers, who have recently started out in the profession. They are in search of acceptance from their students, and therefore they become too friendly with them. They consider their students as their friends and so, they give them too much leniency. In doing so, they fail to maintain the professional standard. This approach never worked. It is counterproductive, and it leads to poor management and control in the classroom, disrespect from the students, and low attainment levels. Teachers and students need to respect the boundaries that define their positions. These boundaries are there for a reason.

The second type of negative student-teacher relationship is physically non-sexual. Nevertheless, it is improper. It happens when teachers, whether experienced or non-experienced, fail to keep a distance from their students. The teachers get too close and personal with the students. Whenever the relationship does not serve the interests of the students, then something is definitely wrong. Teachers are meant to be good role models for their students.

In the second type of negative relationship, the teachers tend to flirt with the students and get involved in inappropriate conversations with them. This process is facilitated by social media and electronic devices like mobile devices and computers. Messages and emails are sent and received between the teachers and students every day. Most of these communications are appropriate, however, some of the teachers send inappropriate messages to students and misuse their conduct of communication. The third type of negative teacher-student relationship is when the students are convinced that the teachers do not care about them and are not concerned whether the students fail or pass. These students do not trust their teachers, and therefore, they seek help elsewhere. For these types of students, teachers need to show care and concern for them on a daily basis and treat them with extra care.

The fourth type of negative relationship takes place when the teachers get involved in sexual relationships with the students. If the student is a minor, then the teacher is guilty of sexual assault. This is categorized as statutory rape. Teachers conducting such behavior end up getting fired from their jobs as well as they face criminal charges in courts. On the contrary, if the student has reached the age of sexual consent, the teacher will only be fired from the job due to sexual misconduct and breach of ethics.

Unethical behavior is a problem that has been growing vastly lately. It has grown to the extent that different state departments of education all over the United States are establishing offices to deal solely with violators of the educator's law. Most of the state departments of education and local schools have established the *"Educators' Code of Ethics."*

The Educators' Code of Ethics was developed by the Association of American Educators (AAE) Advisory Board and by the Executive Committee of the AAE. It contains four basic principles that relate to the rights of the students and the educators.

Principle I: Ethical Conduct towards Students

The professional educator accepts the responsibility to teach students different character qualities that would help them in evaluating the consequences of their actions and learn to accept responsibility for their actions and their choices. Parents are the primary educators of their children. However, we believe that educators are obliged to build virtues like integrity, responsibility, loyalty, and respect for the law, diligence, cooperation, fidelity, and respect for other people and for themselves.

The professional educator accepts his position as a figure of public trust and as someone who measures success not only with the progress of each student but also as a citizen of the community.

Principle II: Ethical Conduct toward Practices and Performance

The educator accepts responsibility and accountability of his/her performance and works even harder to stay competent. A professional educator is one who maintains the dignity of the profession by obeying the law and by demonstrating integrity.

Principle III: Ethical Conduct toward Professional Colleagues

The professional educator deals with justice and treats all the members of the profession equally. S/he does not reveal confidential information that involves a concerning colleague. S/he also does not make false statements about a colleague or about the school system s/he is involved with.

Principle IV: Ethical Conduct toward Parents and Community

The professional educator ensures to protect public power over public education and private control over private education. The professional educator recognizes that education is to be of quality and it is the common goal of the public, the board of education, and the educators, that it is to be achieved. Please get a copy of your state or district's code of ethics for educators and be very familiar with them. Some violations committed by educators are simply because they did not know the behavior was wrong; however, ignorance is no excuse when these documents exist for the safety of adults and children.

Technology in Schools and Ethics

Technology is everywhere. It is also present in schools. When talking about the use of technology in schools, we refer to access to computers and the use of electronic communication like e-mails and social media.

Technology has the ability to change the way teachers teach and improve the outcomes of students. Technology can never become a substitute for interaction, and therefore, it should be used carefully. However, with the benefits of technology, there are also a number of serious and ethical matters that need to be taken into consideration.

The first priority of any school should be to protect the welfare of the students. There are a number of risks that are associated with the use of technology. These include matters of privacy, data security, class communication, cyberbullying, and questionable material.

Data Security

It is about keeping a student's information private and safe. Students can get tempted to put their information on the internet by completing forms and signing up for websites. This is dangerous for their personal security. It is hard for teachers to control students' behavior but blocking dangerous websites and creating awareness amongst students about the risks may be the initial step to take. Schools that collect information through electronic means need to ensure that their security is the chief priority, and they should protect the data that the students have provided.

Privacy

It is related to data security, but it is also related to protecting the students' rights to their own personal lives. Students need to be free to express themselves without someone being a watchman over their shoulders.

Cyberbullying

This is when other students bully students through electronic media. This can be in the form of verbal bullying, insults, and threats. It can also include pictures that are posted online and can cause a threat to the student's reputation. Cyberbullying can further lead to psychological scarring, which triggers students to commit suicides. This should be taken seriously.

Class Communication

This is something that needs to be considered for the protection of students as well as teachers. Nowadays, it is important for teachers to be in communication with students electronically. However, these communications should take place through the systems of the school and not through personal e-mails or personal texting. Professionalism is required at all times. Moreover, communication with the students should be done during school hours and under surveillance in order to keep both the students and teachers safe.

It is crucial that the principal communicates the ethical use of technology. When sending e-mails, text messages, etc., nothing is ever deleted. Everything can be traced back to the sender, as well as the websites accessed through school computers. It is imperative that educators remember this when considering communicating with students and/or other adults inappropriately. Again, this is a serious matter.

This cannot be emphasized enough. Some of the cases of adults behaving unethically are appalling and have a lasting effect on the students who may have been involved. This can ruin a teacher's career and make it very difficult for them to obtain employment in the future.

Role of the Principal in Sexual Misconduct Investigations

Once the head of the school receives information regarding a rumor, or suspected sexual misconduct is occurring in the school, s/he needs to take the necessary measures to get to the bottom of the situation. Once the head has gathered the facts to the situation, s/he needs to immediately inform the chair of the board of trustees and the legal counsel of the situation.

Sexual misconduct is a serious matter that needs to be taken seriously right away as the rights of the victim and the accused are at stake. If the school has a dedicated crisis response team (which I highly recommend) then the team should work to evaluate the situation and take the responsive steps to address the situation. The initial goal of the school is to take the appropriate measures to ensure the well-being of the students and to ensure their safety.

The head of the school also needs to take immediate action to address the situation completely. The head of the school should take the following steps:

- Conduct an investigation in order to gather all of the necessary and important facts. This can be done in cooperation with the police. The police will investigate which may lead to criminal charges;

- Monitor the well-being of the alleged victim and address his/her interests;

- Manage communications properly. Take care of what should be communicated to the victim and the victim's parents or legal guardian. Whatever steps are taken, they should be communicated to the school staff, other students, board members, other families, and the local community;

- Understand all of the documents gathered such as employee handbooks, employment contracts, and written procedures to evaluate what policies (if any) have been violated;

- Follow up with the local police, the victim, the board chair, the legal counsel, the victim's parents, and any other members who may be involved.

- Take whatever action is needed as per the allegations. All the steps taken need to be recorded in documents.

- Once the situation has cleared and calmed down, it is recommended that the principal, the school's leadership team and the legal counsel conduct a briefing session to discuss how the situation occurred, and how it was handled, and what changes have been brought to the school's code of conduct.

Lastly, it is to be added that teachers hold a position of trust. Parents believe in teachers as well as the entire school administration, and therefore embraces that the education of their children is in the responsible hands of the school. It is up to the teachers to completely guide the students to become responsible and successful citizens in the future. Therefore, teachers and administrators should never compromise on their duty and should never ruin the image, which they have created. But most importantly, they should not let the students' image be affected as well. It is only when they will stand proud to the statement, *"All professions can boast, but the teacher is one who taught them all."*

Bibliography

CMS Wire (2018). *4 Ways to Improve Your Data-Driven Decision Making.* Retrieved from https://www.cmswire.com/analytics/4-ways-to-improve-your-data-driven-decision-making/

CMS Wire (2018). *4 Ways to Improve Your Data-Driven Decision Making.* Retrieved from https://www.cmswire.com/analytics/4-ways-to-improve-your-data-driven-decision-making/

CHA World School (2018). *The Importance of Incorporating Technology into Student Education from an Early Age.* Retrieved from https://chaschool.org/importance-incorporating-technology-student-education-early-age/

Capella University (2018). *5 Reasons to Incorporate Technology into Your Classroom.* Retrieved from https://www.capella.edu/blogs/cublog/benefits-of-technology-in-the-classroom/

Seen (2018). *The Principal's Role as Technology Leader.*
Retrieved from
https://www.seenmagazine.us/Articles/Article-
Detail/articleid/1800/the-principal-8217-s-role-as-
technology-leader

EdTech Review (2018). *Roles & Responsibilities of a
School Leader in Technology Integration.* Retrieved
from http://edtechreview.in/trends-
insights/insights/2541-role-of-school-leader-
principal-in-school-technology

EdTech Review (2018). *How Can Technology Make School
Administrators More Productive?* Retrieved from
http://edtechreview.in/news/794-how-can-
technology-make-school-administrators-more-
productive

Education World (2018). *The Administrator's Role in
Technology Integration.* Retrieved from
https://www.educationworld.com/a_tech/tech087.sh
tml

The Voki Blog – Expanding Education (2017). *How to Use
Technology in Teaching and Learning Effectively?*
Retrieved from

https://blog.voki.com/2017/07/28/how-to-use-technology-in-teaching-and-learning-effectively/

Edutopia (2018). *Why Do We Need Technology Integration?* Retrieved from https://www.edutopia.org/technology-integration-guide-importance

eLearning Industry (2018). *Why Integrating Technology in The Classroom Can Better Connect Parents, Teachers, and Students.* Retrieved from https://elearningindustry.com/integrating-technology-in-the-classroom-connect

Education-Colleges.com (2018). *Administration: The Role and Duties of a School Administrator.* Retrieved from https://www.education-colleges.com/administration.html#context/api/listings/prefilter

Australian Children's Education & Care Quality Authority™ (2018). *Educational Leadership.* Retrieved from https://www.acecqa.gov.au/resources/educational-leadership

Top Education Degrees (2017). *What is Educational Leadership?* Retrieved from https://www.topeducationdegrees.org/faq/what-is-educational-leadership/

Education-Colleges.com (2018). *Administration: The Role and Duties of a School Administrator.* Retrieved from https://www.education-colleges.com/administration.html#context/api/listings/prefilter

Wise Toast (2019). *12 Different Types of Leadership Styles.* Retrieved from https://wisetoast.com/12-different-types-of-leadership-styles/

The Wallace Foundation® (2019). *The Principal as Leader: An Overview – The School Principal as Leader: Guiding Schools to Better Teaching and Learning.* Retrieved from https://www.wallacefoundation.org/knowledge-center/pages/overview-the-school-principal-as-leader.aspx

The Wallace Foundation® (2019). *The Principal as Leader: An Overview – The School Principal as Leader: Guiding Schools to Better Teaching and Learning.* Retrieved from https://www.wallacefoundation.org/knowledge-

center/pages/overview-the-school-principal-as-
leader.aspx

ThoughtCo. (2018). *The Role of the Principal in Schools*.
Retrieved from https://www.thoughtco.com/role-of-
principal-in-schools-3194583

ThoughCo. (2018). *10 Things a Successful School
Principal Does Differently*. Retrieved from
https://www.thoughtco.com/things-a-successful-
school-principal-does-differently-3194532

LinkedIn (2018). *Dispositions of Highly Effective School
Leaders*. Retrieved from
https://www.linkedin.com/pulse/dispositions-
highly-effective-school-leaders-bobby-moore

University of San Diego (2019). *10 Traits of Successful
School Leaders*. Retrieved from
https://onlinedegrees.sandiego.edu/effective-
educational-leadership/

Wise Toast (2019). *12 Different Types of Leadership Styles*.
Retrieved from https://wisetoast.com/12-different-
types-of-leadership-styles/

Wise Toast (2019). *12 Different Types of Leadership Styles*.
Retrieved from https://wisetoast.com/12-different-
types-of-leadership-styles/

Wise Toast (2019). *12 Different Types of Leadership Styles.* Retrieved from https://wisetoast.com/12-different-types-of-leadership-styles/

Verywell Mind (2019). *What is Democratic Leadership?* Retrieved from https://www.verywellmind.com/what-is-democratic-leadership-2795315

Wise Toast (2019). *12 Different Types of Leadership Styles.* Retrieved from https://wisetoast.com/12-different-types-of-leadership-styles/

SearchCIO (2019). *Strategic Leadership.* Retrieved from https://searchcio.techtarget.com/definition/strategic-leadership

Wise Toast (2019). *12 Different Types of Leadership Styles.* Retrieved from https://wisetoast.com/12-different-types-of-leadership-styles/

Verywell Mind (2019). *Transformational Leadership.* Retrieved from https://www.verywellmind.com/what-is-transformational-leadership-2795313

Wise Toast (2019). *12 Different Types of Leadership Styles.* Retrieved from https://wisetoast.com/12-different-types-of-leadership-styles/

Wise Toast (2019). *12 Different Types of Leadership Styles.* Retrieved from https://wisetoast.com/12-different-types-of-leadership-styles/

Wise Toast (2019). *12 Different Types of Leadership Styles.* Retrieved from https://wisetoast.com/12-different-types-of-leadership-styles/

Wise Toast (2019). *12 Different Types of Leadership Styles.* Retrieved from https://wisetoast.com/12-different-types-of-leadership-styles/

Wise Toast (2019). *12 Different Types of Leadership Styles.* Retrieved from https://wisetoast.com/12-different-types-of-leadership-styles/

Wise Toast (2019). *12 Different Types of Leadership Styles.* Retrieved from https://wisetoast.com/12-different-types-of-leadership-styles/

TeamWork Definition Information (2017). *What is Charismatic Leadership?* Retrieved from http://teamworkdefinition.com/charismaticleadership/

The Glossary of Education Reform (2014). *Curriculum.* Retrieved from https://www.edglossary.org/curriculum/

The Glossary of Education Reform (2014). *Curriculum.*
Retrieved from
https://www.edglossary.org/curriculum/

ASCD® (2019). *Educational Leadership.* Retrieved from
http://www.ascd.org/publications/educational-
leadership/nov17/vol75/num03/Reimagining-the-
Null-Curriculum.aspx

The Second Principle (2019). *Types of Curriculum.*
Retrieved from
https://thesecondprinciple.com/instructional-
design/types-of-curriculum/

Study Lecture Notes (2017). *Functions of Curriculum in
Education.* Retrieved from
http://www.studylecturenotes.com/curriculum-
instructions/functions-of-curriculum-in-education

Teamwork Definition (2017). *What is Instructional
Leadership?* Retrieved from
http://teamworkdefinition.com/instructionalleadersh
ip/

Working at the Edge (2019). *Vision for Learning.* Retrieved
from http://workingattheedge.org/about/vision/

Training (2019). *Leaders Build Community.* Retrieved from
    https://trainingmag.com/trgmag-article/leaders-
    build-community/

Civil Eats (2013). *To Build Community Leadership,
    Redefine the Meaning of Leadership.* Retrieved
    from https://civileats.com/2013/07/10/to-build-
    community-leadership-redefine-the-meaning-of-
    leadership/

ASCD® (2019). *What is Teacher Leadership?* Retrieved
    from
    http://www.ascd.org/publications/books/105048/cha
    pters/What-Is-Teacher-Leadership%C2%A2.aspx

PennState College of Agricultural Sciences (2019). *What is
    Community Engagement?* Retrieved from
    https://aese.psu.edu/research/centers/cecd/engageme
    nt-toolbox/engagement/what-is-community-
    engagement

Crowe (2018). *The Importance of Stakeholder Engagement.*
    Retrieved from http://www.crowe.ie/importance-
    stakeholder-engagement/

Better Evaluation (2018). *Understand and Engage
    Stakeholders.* Retrieved from

https://www.betterevaluation.org/en/rainbow_frame
work/manage/understand_engage_stakeholders

Teach (2018). *Engaging the Local Community Inside the
School Walls.* Retrieved from
https://teach.com/blog/engaging-the-local-
community-inside-the-school-walls/

Concordia University Portland (2019). *5 Great Ways
Schools Can Engage the Community.* Retrieved
from https://education.cu-
portland.edu/blog/curriculum-teaching-strategies/5-
great-ways-schools-can-engage-the-community/

Pride Surveys (2019). *Why Community Involvement in
Schools is Important.* Retrieved from
https://www.pridesurveys.com/index.php/blog/com
munity-involvement-in-schools/

IDRA (2003). *Community and Public Engagement in
Education-Opportunity and Challenge.* Retrieved
from https://www.idra.org/resource-
center/community-and-public-engagement-in-
education/

Got Core Values (2019). *So Why Is Culture in Schools So
Important?* Retrieved from
http://gotcorevalues.com/culture-schools-important/

Got Core Values (2019). *So Why Is Culture in Schools So Important?* Retrieved from http://gotcorevalues.com/culture-schools-important/

Campus Safety (2019). *31 Steps to a Crisis Management Plan.* Retrieved from https://www.campussafetymagazine.com/emergenc y/crisis-management-plan/

K12 Engagement (2016). *School Climate & Culture.* Retrieved from https://k12engagement.unl.edu/strategy-briefs/School%20Climate%20&%20Culture%202-6-16_1.pdf

School Climate (2007). *School Climate Research Summary.* Retrieved from https://www.schoolclimate.org/storage/app/media/P DF/sc-brief-v3.pdf

Pride Surveys (2019). *What is a School Climate Survey?* Retrieved from https://www.pridesurveys.com/index.php/blog/what -school-climate-survey-teacher-student-measures/

Greater Good Magazine (2019). *How to Create a Positive School Climate.* Retrieved from

https://greatergood.berkeley.edu/article/item/how_t
o_create_a_positive_school_climate

School Leaders Now (2018). *8 Ways Principals Can Build
Positive School Culture Now.* Retrieved from
https://schoolleadersnow.weareteachers.com/8-
ways-build-positive-school-culture-now/

Greater Good Magazine (2019). *How to Create a Positive
School Climate.* Retrieved from
https://greatergood.berkeley.edu/article/item/how_t
o_create_a_positive_school_climate

ED Direct (2015). *Ethics in Education.* Retrieved from
http://www.eddirect.com/resources/education/ethics
-in-education

Professional Standards and Practices Commission (2019).
The Teacher/Student Relationship. Retrieved from
https://www.pspc.education.pa.gov/Promoting-
Ethical-Practices-Resources/Ethics-
Toolkit/Unit3/Pages/The-Teacher---Student-
Relationship.aspx

Professional Standards and Practices Commission (2019).
The Teacher/Student Relationship. Retrieved from
https://www.pspc.education.pa.gov/Promoting-
Ethical-Practices-Resources/Ethics-

Toolkit/Unit3/Pages/The-Teacher---Student-Relationship.aspx

Eduflow (2019). *Negative Teacher-Student Relationships.* Retrieved from https://eduflow.wordpress.com/2014/05/06/negative-teacher-student-relationships/

Association of American Educators (2018). *Code of Ethics for Educators.* Retrieved from https://www.aaeteachers.org/index.php/about-us/aae-code-of-ethics

Study.com (2019). *Ethical Guidelines for Technology Use in Schools.* Retrieved from https://study.com/academy/lesson/ethical-guidelines-for-technology-use-in-schools.html

Studentshubgh (2019). *Sexual Relationship between Teachers and Students: The Cause and the way forward.* Retrieved from https://www.studentshubgh.com/sexual-relationship-between-teachers-and-students/

Guidelines for dealing with educator sexual misconduct (2012) Retrieved from http://www.nais.org/Articles/Documents/Member/E

ducator_Sexual_Misconduct_12_finaledits.pdf?_cld
ee=YnVybmV0dEBuYWlzLm9yZw%3D%3D

Made in the USA
Coppell, TX
16 April 2020

20001126R00154